# GOD'S AMBASSADORS IN JAPAN

by DAN WOODING

## THE KENNY & LILA JOSEPH
*Story*

RIPE PUBLISHING

# *Also by Dan Wooding*

A Light To India (with Lillian Doerksen)
Brother Andrew
God's Smuggler to China (with Brother David and Sarah Bruce)
Junkies are People Too
Stresspoint
I Thought Terry Dene Was Dead
Exit The Devil (with Trevor Dearing)
Train of Terror (with Mini Loman)
Rick Wakeman, the Caped Crusader
King Squealer (with Maurice O'Mahoney)
Farewell Leicester Square (with Henry Hollis)
Uganda Holocaust (with Ray Barnett)
Miracles in Sin City (with Howard Cooper)
Prophets of Revolution (with Peter Asael Gonzales)
Guerilla for Christ (with Salu Daka Ndebele)
Million Dollar Promise (with Duane Logsdon)
Twenty-Six Lead Soldiers
Secret Missions
Singing In The Dark (with Barry Taylor)
Lost for Words (with Stuart Mill)
Let There Be Light (with Roger Oakland)
Rock Priest (with David Pierce)
He Intends Victory
Only Believe (with Hannu Haukka)
Blind Faith (with Anne Wooding)
Never Say Never
From Tabloid to Truth

# *Acknowledgments*

As I thought about who would be the best person to put our parents story to paper, Dan Wooding kept coming to mind. Years ago Dan and I had been on a panel together discussing issues related to journalism and had kept in touch over the years. In 2007 we both hosted TV shows on the same internet based television station. It soon became clear to me that Dan was the perfect person to author this book because he loves God, loves missionaries and loves telling their stories. The depth and breadth of his work-from British tabloids to religious periodicals-means that he understands both the worlds of hardball journalism and missionary work and has brought those sensibilities to this work. I am also grateful to to William F. Turner for his financial commitment toward making this book a reality. Also, my assistants Laura Kobzeff, Yee Sum Lo, Rachelle Klemme, Brooke Anderson, Ronnie Gonzales and Toni Burge all contributed mightily to this book and Bill Sardi was gracious in making Linda available to design the cover.

As I look back on my parents' lives and work in Japan, I am continually reminded of the sacrifice they made to be there. As a father of daughters, in particular I think of my grandfather Olaf Finsaas whom God blessed with just one daughter out of nine children-and the incredible sacrifice he made when he watched his only daughter get on that train and take the first step in a long journey that would for all practical purposes take her out of his life on this earth. Eight short years later he was gone-felled by a heart attack. His sacrifice for the sake of the Gospel was great. But one day there will be a joyous reunion where he will meet not only his daughter again, but the many people who will be with them because of *his* sacrifice and *her* service. May this book inspire each of us to live our lives to the fullest and without regret.

                                      Mark Joseph
                                      May 1, 2009

Ripe Publishing
Los Angeles, California

©2009 Bully! Pulpit Books

All rights reserved. No part of this book may be reproduced in any form without written permission from Ripe Publishing.

Requests for information can be addressed to Info@BullyPulpitBooks.com

Cover design: Linda Tazberikova
Interior design: Toni Burge, Ronnie Gonzales
Editorial assistance:
Yee Sum Lo
Rachelle Klemme
Brooke Anderson
Laura Kobzeff

ISBN 978-0-9824869-0-0

Printed in the United States of America

For more information visit:
*KennyJoseph.com*
*LilaJoseph.com*
*ReapMission.com*
*ReapMagazine.com*

# Contents

| | |
|---|---|
| Chapter 1: Winds of War | 7 |
| Chapter 2: The Eastern Cross | 21 |
| Chapter 3: Kenny Joseph's Long and Winding Road to Japan | 27 |
| Chapter 4: Lila from the Prairie | 43 |
| Chapter 5: A Big Surprise in the Land of the Rising Sun | 65 |
| Chapter 6: Family Life and Parenting | 71 |
| Chapter 7: Philosophy of Missions | 109 |
| Chapter 8: Women's Ministry | 117 |
| Chapter 9: The Great Commission is in Japanese, Too! | 125 |
| Chapter 10: Trouble and Transformation | 141 |
| Chapter 11: Life in The Land of The Rising Sun | 151 |
| Chapter 12: The Josephs – Today and Beyond | 173 |
| Appendix 1 | 185 |
| Appendix 2 | 191 |
| Appendix 3 | 195 |
| About the Author | 200 |

# Chapter 1

# *Winds of War*

The face of U.S. President Franklin Delano Roosevelt was ashen as he addressed his nation on Monday, December 8th, 1941, about the surprise Japanese attack on Pearl Harbor, Hawaii.

As millions of Americans gathered around their radios across their vast land, the 32nd President of the United States began a speech that reverberated around the world: "Yesterday, December 7th, 1941 – a date which will live in infamy – the United States of America was suddenly and deliberately attacked by Naval and Air forces of the Empire of Japan. The United States was at peace with that nation and, at the solicitation of Japan, was still in conversation with its government and its Emperor looking toward the maintenance of peace in the Pacific. Indeed, one hour after Japanese air squadrons had commenced bombing in the American island of Oahu, the Japanese ambassador to the United States and his colleague delivered to our Secretary of State a formal reply to a recent American message. And while this reply stated that it seemed useless to continue the existing diplomatic negotiations, it contained no threat or hint of war or of armed attack. It will be recorded that the distance of Hawaii from Japan makes it obvious that the attack was deliberately planned many weeks ago. During the intervening time, the Japanese government has deliberately sought to deceive the United States by false statements and expressions of hope for continued peace. The attack yesterday on the Hawaiian Islands has caused severe damage to American naval and military forces. I regret to tell you that very many American lives have been lost."

The US government's National Archives and Records Administration described the drama of that day in this way, "Early in the afternoon of December 7th, 1941, President Franklin D. Roosevelt and his chief foreign policy aide, Harry Hopkins, were interrupted by a telephone call from Secretary of War Henry Stimson and told that the Japanese had attacked Pearl Harbor. At about 5:00 p.m., following meetings with his military advisers, the President calmly and decisively dictated to his secretary, Grace Tully, a request to Congress for a declaration of war. He had composed the speech in his head after deciding on a brief, uncomplicated appeal to the people of the United States rather than a thorough recitation of Japanese perfidies, as Secretary of State Cordell Hull had urged.

"President Roosevelt then revised the typed draft—marking it up, updating military information, and selecting alternative wordings that strengthened the tone of the speech. He made the most significant change in the critical first line, which originally read, 'a date which will live in world history.' Grace Tully then prepared the final reading copy, which Roosevelt subsequently altered in three more places.

"On December 8th, at 12:30 p.m., Roosevelt addressed a joint session of Congress and the Nation via radio. The Senate responded with a unanimous vote in support of war; only Montana pacifist Jeanette Rankin dissented in the House. At 4:00 p.m. that same afternoon, President Roosevelt signed the declaration of war."

The document went on to say, "Roosevelt misplaced his reading copy immediately following the speech; it remained missing for 43 years. Instead of bringing the reading copy back to the White House for Grace Tully to file, the President evidently left it in the House chamber, where he had given the address. A Senate clerk took charge of it, endorsed it 'Dec. 8th, 1941, Read in joint session,' and filed it. In March 1984 an archivist located the reading copy among the Records of the U.S. Senate, Record Group 46, located in the National Archives building, where it remains today."

Up until that time, the American people had stayed out of World War II. Now that there was no alternative but to join with the Allied Forces and enter the war against Japan in Asia and the Axis Powers in Europe. The attack on Pearl Harbor, or "Hawaii Operation" as it was called by the Imperial General Headquarters, was a surprise attack against the United States by the Japanese Navy whose secret code was "Tora, Tora, Tora!" translated into English as "Tiger, Tiger, Tiger!"

The attack was intended as a preventative action by Japan to remove the U.S. Pacific Fleet as a factor in the war they were about to wage against Britain, the Netherlands, and the United States. 2,388 American soldiers were killed and 1,178 wounded in the attack. The aim of the strike was to protect Imperial Japan's advance into Malaya and the Dutch East Indies — for their natural resources such as oil and rubber — by neutralizing the U.S. Pacific Fleet. Both the U.S. and Japan had long-standing contingency plans for war in the Pacific, continuously updated as tension between the two countries steadily increased during the 1930s.

A report by the Department Of The Navy – Naval Historical Center, Washington Navy Yard – noted the following: "The December 7$^{th}$, 1941 Japanese raid on Pearl Harbor was one of the great defining moments in history. A single carefully-planned and well-executed stroke removed the United States Navy's battleship force as a possible threat to the Japanese Empire's southward expansion. America, unprepared and now considerably weakened, was abruptly brought into the Second World War as a full combatant."

With Roosevelt's declaration of war, America once again found itself engaged in a world war which would continue for nearly four years against a tenacious enemy. All the while America was working to develop a nuclear weapon which was deployed after six months of intense firebombing of 67 other Japanese cities. The atomic weapon "Little Boy" was dropped on war factories in the city of Hiroshima on Monday, August 6$^{th}$, 1945, followed on August 9$^{th}$ by the detonation of a second nuclear bomb, "Fat Man" over the city of Nagasaki. These are to date the only attacks with nuclear weapons in the history of warfare, and the bombs killed as many as 140,000 people in Hiroshima and 80,000 in Nagasaki by the end of 1945, with roughly half dying on the days of the bombings. Since then, thousands more have died from injuries or illnesses attributed to exposure to radiation released by the bombs. In both cities, the overwhelming majority of the dead were civilians, but both cities were picked because of their many factories of war.

The US Department of Energy described what happened during the Atomic Bombing of Hiroshima this way:

"In the early morning hours of August 6$^{th}$, 1945, a B-29 bomber named *Enola Gay* took off from the island of Tinian and headed north by northwest toward Japan. The bomber's primary target was the city of Hiroshima, located on the deltas of southwestern Honshu Island facing the Inland Sea. Hiroshima had a civilian population of almost 300,000 and was an important military center, containing about 43,000 soldiers. The bomber, piloted by the commander of the 509th Composite Group, Colonel Paul Tibbets, flew at low altitude on automatic pilot before climbing to 31,000 feet as it neared the target area. At approximately 8:15 a.m. Hiroshima time, the *Enola Gay* released 'Little Boy,' its 9,700-pound uranium bomb, over the city. Tibbets immediately dove away to avoid the anticipated shock wave. Forty-three seconds later, a huge explosion lit the morning sky as Little Boy detonated 1,900 feet above the city, directly over a parade field where soldiers of the Japanese Second Army were doing calisthenics. Though already eleven and a half miles away, the *Enola Gay* was rocked by the blast. At first, Tibbets thought he was taking flak. After a second shock wave hit the plane, the crew looked back at Hiroshima. "The city was hidden by that awful cloud...boiling up, mushrooming, terrible and incredibly tall," Tibbets recalled. The yield of the explosion was later estimated at fifteen kilotons (the equivalent of 15,000 tons of TNT).

"On the ground, moments before the blast, it was a calm and sunny Monday morning. An air raid alert from earlier that morning had been called off after only a solitary aircraft was seen, and by 8:15 the city was alive with activity – soldiers doing their morning calisthenics, commuters on foot or on bicycles, groups of women and children working outside to clear firebreaks. Those closest to the explosion died instantly, their bodies turned to black char. Nearby birds burst into flames in mid-air, and dry, combustible materials such as paper instantly ignited as far away as 6,400 feet from ground zero. The white light acted as a giant flashbulb, burning the dark patterns of clothing onto skin and the shadows of bodies onto walls. Survivors outdoors close to the blast generally describe a literally blinding light combined with a sudden and overwhelming wave of heat. The blast wave followed almost instantly for those close in, often knocking them from their feet. Those that were indoors were usually spared the flash burns, but flying glass from broken windows filled most rooms, and all but the very strongest structures collapsed. One boy was blown through the windows of his house and across the street as the house collapsed behind him. Within minutes, nine out of ten people half a mile or less from ground zero were dead.

"People farther from the point of detonation experienced first the flash and heat, followed seconds later by a deafening boom and the blast wave. Nearly every structure within one mile of ground zero was destroyed, and almost every building within three miles was damaged. Less than ten percent of the buildings in the city survived without any damage, and the blast wave shattered glass in suburbs twelve miles away. The most common first reaction of those that were indoors even miles from ground zero was that their building had just suffered a direct hit by a bomb. Small ad hoc rescue parties soon began to operate, but roughly half of the city's population was dead or injured. In those areas most seriously affected, virtually no one escaped serious injury. The numerous small fires that erupted simultaneously all around the city soon merged into one large fire storm, creating extremely strong winds that blew towards the center of the fire. The fire storm eventually engulfed 4.4 square miles of the city, killing anyone who had not escaped in the first minutes after the attack. One postwar study of the victims of Hiroshima found that less than 4.5 percent of survivors suffered leg fractures. Such injuries were not uncommon; it was just that most who could not walk were engulfed by the fire storm.

"Even after the flames had subsided, relief from the outside was slow in coming. For hours after the attack the Japanese government did not even know for sure what had happened. Radio and telegraph communications with Hiroshima had suddenly ended at 8:16 a.m., and vague reports of some sort of large explosion had begun to filter in, but the Japanese high command knew that no large-scale air raid had taken place over the city and that there were no large stores of explosives there. Eventually a Japanese staff officer was dispatched by plane to survey the city from overhead. While he was still nearly 100 miles away from the city, he began to report on a huge cloud of smoke that hung over it. The first confirmation of exactly what had happened came only sixteen hours later with the announcement of the bombing by the United States.

"At 11:00 a.m., August 6th (Washington D.C. time), radio stations began playing a prepared statement from President Truman informing the American public that the United States had dropped an entirely new type of bomb on Hiroshima – an atomic bomb. Truman warned that if Japan still refused to surrender unconditionally, as demanded by the Potsdam Declaration of July 26th, the United States would attack additional targets with equally devastating results. Two days later, on August 8th, the Soviet Union declared war on Japan and attacked Japanese forces in Manchuria, ending American hopes that the war would end before Russian entry into the Pacific theater. By August 9th, American aircraft were showering leaflets all over Japan informing its people that 'We are in possession of the most destructive explosive ever devised by man. A single one of our newly developed atomic bombs is actually the equivalent in explosive power to what 2,000 of our giant B-29's can carry on a single mission. This awful fact is one for you to ponder and we solemnly assure you it is grimly accurate. We have just begun to use this weapon against your homeland. If you still have any doubt, make inquiry as to what happened to Hiroshima when just one atomic bomb fell on that city.'

The document continued: "Meanwhile, Tibbett's bomber group was simply waiting for the weather to clear in order to drop its next bomb, the plutonium weapon nicknamed 'Fat Man' which was destined for the city of Nagasaki.

"The next break in the weather over Japan was due to appear just three days after the attack on Hiroshima, to be followed by at least five more days of prohibitive weather. The plutonium bomb, nicknamed 'Fat Man,' was rushed into readiness to take advantage of this window. No further orders were required for the attack. Truman's order of July 25th had authorized the dropping of additional bombs as soon as they were ready. At 3:47 a.m. on August 9th, 1945, a B-29 named Bock's Car lifted off from Tinian and headed toward the primary target: Kokura Arsenal, a massive collection of war industries adjacent to the city of Kokura.

"From this point on, few things went according to plan. The aircraft commander, Major Charles W. Sweeney, ordered the arming of the bomb only ten minutes after takeoff so that the aircraft could be pressurized and climb above the lightning and squalls that menaced the flight all the way to Japan. Sweeney then discovered that, due to a minor malfunction, he would not be able to access his reserve fuel. The aircraft next had to orbit the city of Yokohama for almost an hour in order to rendezvous with its two escort B-29s, one of which never arrived."

The document stated that the weather had been reported "satisfactory" earlier in the day over Kokura Arsenal, but by the time the B-29 finally arrived there, the target was obscured by smoke and haze. Two more passes over the target still produced no sightings of the aiming point. As an aircraft crewman Jacob Beser later recalled, Japanese fighters and bursts of antiaircraft fire were by this time starting to make things "a little hairy." Kokura no longer appeared to be an option, and there was only enough fuel on board to return to the secondary airfield on Okinawa, making one hurried pass as they went over their secondary target: the city of Nagasaki. As Beser later put it, "there was no sense dragging the bomb home or dropping it in the ocean."

As it turned out, cloud cover obscured Nagasaki as well. Sweeney reluctantly approved a much less accurate radar approach on the target. At the last moment the bombardier, Captain Kermit K. Beahan, caught a brief glimpse of the city's stadium through the clouds and dropped the bomb. At 11:02 a.m., at an altitude of 1,650 feet, Fat Man exploded over Nagasaki. The yield of the explosion was later estimated at 21 kilotons, 40 percent greater than that of the Hiroshima bomb.

Nagasaki was an industrial center and major port on the western coast of Kyushu. As had happened at Hiroshima, the "all-clear" from an early morning air raid alert had long been given by the time the B-29 had begun its bombing run. A small conventional raid on Nagasaki on August 1st had resulted in a partial evacuation of the city, especially of schoolchildren. There were still almost 200,000 people in the city below the bomb when it exploded. The hurriedly-targeted weapon ended up detonating almost exactly between two of the principal targets in the city, the Mitsubishi Steel and Arms Works to the south, and the Mitsubishi-Urakami Torpedo Works to the north. Had the bomb exploded farther south, the residential and commercial heart of the city would have suffered much greater damage.

"In general," the document said, "though Fat Man exploded with greater force than Little Boy, the damage at Nagasaki was not as great as at Hiroshima. The hills of Nagasaki, its geographic layout, and the bomb's detonation over an industrial area all helped shield portions of the city from the weapon's blast, heat, and radiation effects. The explosion affected a total area of approximately 43 square miles. About 8.5 of those square miles were water, and 33 more square miles were only partially settled. Many roads and rail lines escaped major damage. In some areas electricity was not knocked out, and fire breaks created over the last several months helped to prevent the spread of fires to the south.

"Although the destruction at Nagasaki has generally received less worldwide attention than that at Hiroshima, it was extensive nonetheless. Almost everything up to half a mile from ground zero was completely destroyed, including even the earthquake-hardened concrete structures that had sometimes survived at comparable distances at Hiroshima."

According to a Nagasaki Prefectural Report, "men and animals died almost instantly" within one kilometer (0.62 miles) of the point of detonation. Almost all homes within a mile and a half were destroyed, and dry, combustible materials such as paper instantly burst into flames as far away as 10,000 feet from ground zero. Of the 52,000 homes in Nagasaki, 14,000 were destroyed and 5,400 more seriously damaged. Only 12 percent of the homes escaped unscathed. The official Manhattan Engineer District report on the attack termed the damage to the two Mitsubishi plants "spectacular." Despite the absence of a fire storm, numerous secondary fires erupted throughout the city. Firefighting efforts were hampered by water line breaks, and six weeks later the city was still suffering from a shortage of water.

A U.S. Navy officer who visited the city in mid-September reported that, even over a month after the attack, "a smell of death and corruption pervades the place." As at Hiroshima, the psychological effects of the attack were undoubtedly considerable.

The day after the attack on Nagasaki, the emperor of Japan overruled his military leaders and forced them to offer to surrender unconditionally. Six days after the detonation over Nagasaki, Japan announced its surrender to the Allied Powers, led by General Douglas MacArthur, signing the instruments of surrender on September 2$^{nd}$ on an American battleship, officially ending the Pacific War and therefore World War II. The bombings led, in part, to post-war Japan adopting its Three Non-Nuclear Principles, forbidding that nation from armament and renouncing the use of war forever.

Emperor Hirohito took to the airwaves of Japan where he, in essence, renounced his divinity. In one fell blow, the Shinto religion was left prostrate with no state help, the unseen Buddha had no arms of mercy to extend, and millions of Japanese were left to their own devices.

After the end of the Second World War, Japan was occupied by the Allied Powers led by the United States with contributions from Australia, India, the United Kingdom, and New Zealand. This foreign presence marked the first time since the unification of Japan in 1846 that it was occupied by a foreign power. The San Francisco Peace Treaty, signed on September 8$^{th}$, 1951, marked the end of the Allied occupation. Subsequent to its coming into force on April 28$^{th}$, 1952, Japan was once again an independent state, but with many U.S. military bases.

Japan initially surrendered to the Allies on August 14$^{th}$, 1945, when the Japanese Suzuki government notified the Allies that it had accepted the Potsdam Declaration. On the following day, Emperor Hirohito announced Japan's unconditional surrender on the radio. The announcement was the emperor's first ever radio broadcast and the first time Japanese ever heard his voice. This date is known in the U.S. as Victory Over Japan, or V-J Day, and marked the end of World War II and the beginning of a long road to recovery for a shattered Japan.

On V-J Day, United States President Harry Truman appointed General Douglas MacArthur as Supreme Commander of the Allied Powers (SCAP) to supervise the occupation of Japan. During the war, the Allied Powers had planned to divide Japan amongst themselves for the purposes of occupation, as was done for the occupation of Germany.

Under the final plan, however, SCAP was given direct control over the four main islands of Japan.

Russia invaded Japan in the last week, hoping to rule North Japan, but MacArthur rejected their claim. The Far Eastern Commission and Allied Council for Japan were also established to supervise the Japan occupation. MacArthur arrived in Tokyo on August 30$^{th}$, 1945, and immediately decreed several laws: No Allied personnel were to assault Japanese people. No Allied personnel were to eat the scarce Japanese food. Flying the Hinomaru or "Rising Sun" flag, associated with militarism, was severely restricted. General MacArthur was technically supposed to defer to an advisory council set up by the Allied powers, but in practice, he did everything himself. His first priority was to set up a food distribution network; saying, "send me food or more guns.

"Why? Well, following the collapse of the ruling government and the wholesale destruction of most major cities – 100,000 died in one fire bombing of Tokyo – virtually everyone was starving. Even with these measures, millions of people were still on the brink of starvation for several years after the surrender.

During the early days of the U.S. Occupation, beginning in September 1945, U.S. officials sought to demilitarize and democratize Japan. This meant discarding the schoolbooks that reproduced Shinto myth as history and glorified the Samurai and the heroes of the Sino-Japanese and Russo-Japanese Wars. The American-authored constitution still remains in effect 60 years later. U.S. officials converted the now-cooperative Emperor Hirohito from head of state to "symbol of state" and persuaded him (in his "ningen sengen" or "statement of humanity" on New Year's Day 1946) to publicly renounce claims to divinity. This meant challenging the prevalent religious beliefs and opening the door to aggressive Christian missionary activity, preaching the Gospel nation-wide and distributing Christian tracts.

"In October of 1945, barely a month after he accepted the surrender of Japan on the deck of the USS Missouri, General Douglas MacArthur sat down with a delegation of American clergy at his headquarters in the Dai-Ichi Insurance Building in downtown Tokyo," noted Tim Shorrock in an essay on missionary activity in Japan, Red Flags and Christian Soldiers. "The four churchmen had come to Japan to rekindle a dialogue with Japanese Christians cut short by World War II. They were the first Americans in civilian clothes to enter postwar Japan."

Several German missionaries and five women missionaries were under house arrest or in prison. One Salvation Army missionary died. Supreme Commander Gen. Douglas MacArthur, himself a devout Christian, he sent a telegram to a group known for publishing Bibles, The Gideons, asking for spiritual assistance in the form of Bibles. "I have publicly stated my firm belief that Christianity offers to Japanese a sure and stable foundation on which to build a democratic nation," wrote the General. "Japanese are becoming increasingly aware of fundamental values of Christian religion and appreciative of its spiritual and moral blessing. Your assistance will be of inestimable value. Copies of Holy Scriptures, especially New Testaments, both in English and Japanese, are essential for success of Christian movement as basis for study and acceptance of the faith. Japanese texts more in demand and can be read with fuller comprehension by more people. Your representatives are welcome to come to Japan as missionaries to make firsthand survey of the situation. Information being furnished you by airmail will be helpful for your planning. I assure you of my deep appreciation of your interest in the spiritual rehabilitation of the Japanese people."

To Eric North, the head of the American Bible Society, Macarthur wired: "I have read your report that the American Bible Society, working in conjunction with the Japan Bible Society, has made possible the distribution of more than 4,000,000 copies of the Scriptures since the beginning of the Occupation. My Chaplain... tells me that people of 51 denominations in 48 States have contributed to this project. That your expenditures have now passed the $1,000,000 mark is an indication of the great generosity of the American people and represents a very gratifying achievement. You are well on the way to reaching the goal of 10,000,000 copies which I requested. I confidently believe you will succeed."

"Japan is a spiritual vacuum," he told U.S. Protestant evangelicals visiting Japan in late 1945. "If you do not fill it with Christianity, it will be filled with Communism. Send me 1,000 missionaries."

"So began one of the strangest episodes of the Cold War," noted Shorrock. "MacArthur's attempt to harness Christianity in his mission to transform Japan into an anti-communist and pro-American bastion of democracy. Between 1946 and 1950, over 2,000 American teachers, social workers and evangelists came to Japan in response to a recruitment drive launched by mainstream and evangelical churches and blessed at the highest levels of the U.S. government."

Shorrock, who himself traveled to Japan with his missionary parents, noted of MacArthur's zeal: "'The general had ... a messianic complex – a consciousness of being called of God for the hour and a confidence that God was on his side,' wrote William P. Woodward, a prewar missionary to Japan and author of The Allied Occupation of Japan and Japanese Religions, a history in English of MacArthur's policies and attitudes towards religion.

According to Woodward, who directed the Occupation's Religious Research Unit, MacArthur viewed Japan's traditional religions as inferior and an even dangerous school of thought; only Christianity, he believed, could provide the proper moral foundation Japan must acquire to build a democracy and insulate itself from the communist ideology creeping in from all sides. What Japan needed, MacArthur once declared in a speech quoted by Woodward, was a "spiritual recrudescence and improvement of human character that will synchronize with our almost matchless advance in science, art, literature, and all material and cultural development of the past 2,000 years."

That elegant rhetoric deeply impressed President Truman, who quoted the passage in his official letter of endorsement the American clergymen carried during their visit to Japan."

"When the American churchmen met MacArthur in the fall of 1945, over 160 Japanese cities, including the great industrial centers of Tokyo, Osaka, Yokohama, Kobe, Hiroshima, and Nagasaki were in ruins, the last two by the world's first atomic weapons," observes Shorrock. "Throughout the country, food was scarce. As defeated Japanese soldiers trickled back from their outposts in China, Korea, and the South Pacific, the hungry, exhausted populace left at home ached for rice, vegetables, meat, sustenance. The desperation was keenly felt by the visiting Christians. In meetings with Japanese ministers and lay people, they encountered a confused, dispirited people ashamed of their complicity with militarism, bitter at the terrible American bombing raids that destroyed more than 500 churches and killed countless civilians, and desperate for outside assistance and relief. The people are 'shocked and hurt and humbled and miserable,' a Japanese colleague told them."

The delegation was led by Dr. Douglas Horton, who represented the American Committee for the liberal World Council of Churches, and Dr. Lumar J. Shafer of the Foreign Missions Conference of North America, who had been a teacher at a Tokyo Christian school for eleven years before the war. Their mission, as they summarized it in a 1946 report, adopted MacArthur's convergence of spiritual and political goals. "We came as citizens of a country which was interested in bringing Japan into its own political orbit, yet our chief, in fact, our only purpose was to advance the cause of the church of Christ," they said.

After completing its survey of Japanese churches, the Horton delegation returned to New York and began the task of setting up the missionary effort. Six missionaries who had previously worked in Japan were selected by their churches to work out the procedures with SCAP. They began to recruit volunteers to work in Japan, particularly in Christian schools where, according to a youth magazine published in 1946, the "day to day influence of a Christian life will count for the most."

The first wave of new missionaries came primarily from churches affiliated with the Federal Council of Churches, America's largest coalition of Protestant denominations. Since the days of the "social gospel" of the late 1800s, churches in the council had emphasized social work and education above the task of evangelism and conversion. As part of their social commitment, they had been cooperating with churches in England to send missionaries to Japan, China, and other Asian countries for over a century. But now, with the British Empire in ruins and the United States eclipsing England as a world power, the American churches were suddenly the major source for missionary work overseas.

Most of the volunteers were young people just out of college, Bible school or the military. They were motivated by a raft of postwar concerns: reconciliation with the former enemy, pity for Hiroshima and Nagasaki, and sorrow for the Japanese-Americans assigned to relocation camps. "Conspicuous by its absence was the old, stereotyped missionary jargon such as saving the heathen," wrote a missionary who arrived in 1948 and conducted a survey of missionary attitudes 40 years later.

On May 22nd, 1947, MacArthur's General Headquarters, known as GHQ, announced the liberalization of its entry procedures for missionaries following a meeting with a large group of Catholic and Protestant representatives in Japan. The policy allowed families with children into the country for the first time since the war and authorized the churches to ship tons of food, clothing, prefabricated housing, motor vehicles and other supplies to the new arrivals. "Under this review policy, it is anticipated that the flow of missionaries to Japan within the next three years will be greatly increased," GHQ said in a press release that is stored at the U.S. National Archives in Suitland, Maryland. "This is in line with General MacArthur's desire to encourage Japanese understanding and acceptance of basic principles [of Christianity]. The Supreme Commander seeks to facilitate the entry of as many qualified missionaries as possible."

Among these recruits were a young Chicagoan named Kenny Joseph and a native of Fairview, Montana, named Lila Finsaas, who volunteered to go as missionaries to Japan in 1951 and 1954, respectively, through Youth For Christ and T.E.A.M Mission, one of America's largest mission agencies.

On May 1$^{st}$, 1951, just six short years after hostilities had ceased, Kenny and YFC arrived in Japan on the President Wilson. He began intense language study and soon commenced traveling as an evangelist across Japan. Three years later, Lila also arrived in Japan by ship to begin the life of a single missionary language student – or so she thought. Both were players in a larger "war" – sanctioned by the U.S. government at the highest levels – for the hearts and minds of the Japanese people.

"Going by numbers alone, the American crusade was a miserable failure," noted author Tim Shorrock. "In the political turbulence after World War II, millions of Japanese joined the Japanese Communist Party and aligned themselves with the pacifist Japanese Left to organize and join labor unions and demonstrate against the spread and testing of nuclear weapons. But judged on human terms, the American missionary influx after 1945 was profound; it helped heal the wounds of war and exposed the defeated Japanese to a new kind of American, neither businessman nor soldier, willing to forgo the comforts of home to share the Gospel in the uncertainties and poverty of postwar Japan."

"They were young and idealistic, and identified with Japan," recalls Kiyoko Takeda Cho, a prominent Christian intellectual who lives in Tokyo and was one of my parents' first Japanese friends," noted Shorrock "They represented not the ruling country, but came for preaching and reconciliation. That attitude was very much appreciated, not only by Christians but also non-Christians."

Indeed, what was unique about the post-World War II missionary movement to Japan – and what sets it apart from almost any other missionary campaign of the past 100 years – was its relationship to the government of the "ruling country" that dominated Japan from 1945 to 1952. Unlike Germany, which was divided into four zones by a coalition of allied powers, Japan was under direct control of the U.S. Occupation Army and the Supreme Commander of Allied Forces Pacific, SCAP. From the first day of the occupation, General MacArthur had a mandate from President Truman to take whatever actions he deemed necessary to free Japan from the ideological grip of the "vicious and cruel savages" (Truman's words) who led Japan into the war. To MacArthur, this unprecedented power was a golden opportunity to export "Christianity, American-style."

Kenny Joseph and Lila Finsaas were two foot soldiers in MacArthur's army, but their ultimate allegiance was to the God of the Bible whom they firmly believed had called them to leave the comforts of home and travel to bring the Gospel of Jesus Christ to the people of Japan.

# Chapter 2

# *The Eastern Cross*

Although the Japan that Kenny & Lila encountered had been "freed" from the notion that its Emperor was divine, it was still in the grip of the Shinto religion which had been a major part of Japanese life and culture throughout the country's history. For the greater part of that history, Shinto shared its spiritual, cultural, and political roles with Buddhism.

According to the Religious Tolerance website, Shinto is an ancient Japanese religion. Starting about 500 BCE (or earlier), it was originally "an amorphous mix of nature worship, fertility cults, divination techniques, hero worship, and shamanism."

Its name was derived from the Chinese words "shin tao" ("The Way of the gods"). At that time, The Yamato dynasty consolidated its rule over most of Japan, divine origins were ascribed to the Imperial family, and Shinto established itself as an official religion of Japan, along with Buddhism in the 7$^{th}$ century.

The complete separation of Japanese religion from politics did not occur until just after World War II when the Emperor was forced by the American army to renounce his divinity. Unlike most other religions, Shinto has no real founder, no written scriptures, no body of religious law, and only a very loosely-organized priesthood.

But although Shinto was the most recognized religion in Japan for many years, Christianity was not new to the country, as Kenny Joseph would soon learn. To his surprise, he discovered that the first Christians came to Japan across the Silk Road in 199 A.D. A constant theme in Kenny's work in Japan, and one which would later be picked up by his eldest son Ken, has been his work in tracing the Christian heritage of Japan back to its roots which he believes are in the first and second centuries, not in the 1600s as widely believed today.

It all hinges on one amazing but little-known fact: that Kyoto was not originally a Buddhist city. In fact, the Imperial Family escaped to

Kyoto from Nara when the Buddhists took over in the sixth century. Kyoto was originally an anti-Buddhist city started by those who sought religious freedom.

According to Professor Sakae Ikeda, formerly of Osaka University, and Professor Yoshiro Saeki, formerly of Waseda University, the first Christians came to Japan across the Silk Road sometime in the 2nd century seeking religious freedom. These pilgrims eventually settled in the Kyoto area, and the long Christian history of Kyoto began. Even as Nara became a Buddhist City shortly after the arrival of Buddhism in the 6th century, Kyoto remained adamantly anti-Buddhist and presumably Christian.

Prince Shotoku was the most important person in early Japanese history, a prince in ancient Japan. His real name was "Umayato" which means "door of stable." He was given that name because his mother, Empress Anahobeno-hashinohito, gave birth to him in front of the stable door, thus, his name. He was said to be an intelligent person from childhood, and it was said that he could listen to what ten people were saying, all speaking at once.

Prince Shotoku's great uncle Umako Soga was devoted to Paekche (Kudara) Buddhism. Therefore, it is believed that Prince Umayato was influenced by his Great Uncle and started to learn about Buddhism. However, Prince Umayato was devoted to Buddhism. According to researchers, he studied under two Buddhist priests from Koguryo and Paekche (Korea).

Sushun, who was the uncle of Umayato and a brother of Emperor Youmei and Suiko, took over the throne after Emperor Youmei died. Since he did not like Umako's despotic behavior, he was assassinated by Umako, his uncle. Prince Umayato's aunt became Empress Suiko in 592 A.D. after a competition for the throne between the Soga family and the Mononobe family was settled.

Prince Shotoku sent the first envoy to Sui Dynasty in China; he established an official rank and a constitution. He built two famous temples in Japan, the Shitenno-ji in 593 A.D. and Horyu-ji in 607 A.D. He achieved many things before his mysterious death in 622 A.D.

With the fall of Shotoku Taishi in Nara and his democratic tradition, the city of Kyoto was decimated and the Christians scattered, many going to Yamaguchi and other areas. In the 7th century during Taishi's reign, the center of learning, power and wealth was in Nara. A true democrat, Shotoku Taishi sought to bring balance, including freedom of religion, to his land. Buddhists destroyed this freedom after his death, assassinating two Emperors and driving the Imperial family to escape to Kyoto. At that time, the Hata tribes, descendants of the Christian Keikyo, were wealthy and successful in Kyoto and stood strongly against Buddhism. The Buddhists, however, gained strength, attacking and eventually taking Kyoto along with much of the country, causing the Hata people to disperse all over Japan thereby further spreading Christianity.

When Francis Xavier arrived in Yamaguchi Prefecture in 1550, he was surprised to find that the Keikyo people still held to the idea of Dainichi, or the One Great God. They had forgotten much of the Gospel, but they held on to the Dainichi teaching. Xavier's preaching brought them back to the faith of their fathers. Slowly they began to trickle back to Kyoto. By the year 1593, the quiet good works of the Kirishitan (Christians) in Kyoto had touched so many that Taiko Hideyoshi Toyotomi, the military dictator of Japan, donated a vast area of land to the Church. In August 1594, the construction on this land was completed. The Kirishitan area of Kyoto contained a church, a monastery, and two hospitals, the first in Kyoto. The Kirishitan area of Kyoto, known even today as Deos Alachi, or God's Town, renewed its long Christian past. (Deos is written with the Chinese characters for heavenly lord and spoken with the Latin pronunciation.)

Two years later, in September 1596, an earthquake hit Kyoto wiping out whole areas of the city. Immediately the Kirishitan reached out to the people in need with rescue efforts. Distribution of food, clothing, and other necessities were carried out by the Church.

"With the wholesale deaths of so many, the common people lined up at the gates of the Buddhist temples for help in burying their dead," Kenny later noted. "Not only did the Buddhist temples not respond to the mass of human suffering, they demanded payment before they would perform the funerals. 'We have no money! Everybody is dead! Help us!' they would say.

But only those with money were allowed in the temples' gates. In desperation they sought those who had loved, fed and clothed them. They desperately asked, 'Can you bury our dead? We have no money.'

'Of course!' was the reply of the Kirishitan. Overnight, the simple but revolutionary stories spread through Kyoto like wildfire. The people began to say, 'The Kirishitan fed us, they clothed us, they rescued us and they buried our dead! The God of the Kirishitan is real!'

The concept that God truly cared… turned the city of Kyoto upside down! The temples of Kyoto lay deserted as Myoshanji and the six huge Deos Aachi areas overflowed with the hungry, the poor, the needy and, most of all, the liberated! In a moment the people had seen the oppression and the falseness and…threw off the oppression that had ruled their lives for centuries."

But the Enemy was not so keen to turn over a whole city to the one true God. Immediately the Buddhist priests began to move. Daily they went to Hideyoshi because they now were facing imminent collapse. The lie that said you had to pay for God's favor, pay when somebody died, pay when you lost a child, and forever live under fear of the temple, had been exposed for what it was. Faith in God was free!

Hideyoshi, though he loved the Kirishitan deeply, could not stand against the system that supported his regime. One of the governors of Kyoto named Masuda and a wicked Buddhist priest named Yakuin daily pressured Hideyoshi, who was suffering severe financial ruin as a result of a number of setbacks. Greed won out, and the system triumphed as guards were sent to the Kirishitan areas, and on January 2nd, 1597, the Kirishitan in Kyoto gathered for their last assembly.

While the people were in Church, forty soldiers entered to take them to prison. The next day, six prisoners from Osaka and eighteen from Kyoto were brought together and, with the Buddhist priests cheering, mutilated in front of the people. They were beaten, and a part of the left ear of each one was severed. They were placed on eight oxcarts and paraded through the streets. They traveled from Kyoto to Himeji, then to Sako Shi near the small port where the Christians had originally landed, arriving in Nagasaki on February 4th.

When the martyrs heard the sentence against them – "death on the cross" – they rejoiced and thanked God. One of them delivered a short sermon, in which he said, "Dear brothers in Christ! The intensely desired hour has arrived. Freed from the shackles of our body it is given us to enjoy…the eternal reward. We have experienced how faithful God is in fulfilling His promises, and the end of our sufferings will bring permanent consolation. Let us therefore trust in God and humbly ask of Him the grace to persevere."

On February 5th, 1597, the first of the martyrs were hung on crosses in Nagasaki. The youngest boy, Louis Ibaragi, just twelve years old, refused to renounce his faith. Crowds swarmed the hill at the site of the Martyrs. On the way up the hill, a nobleman tried to persuade young Ibaragi to give up. Instead he turned the other way, looked up the hill and cried out to the astonished crowd, "Where is my cross?"

As the crowd silently wept at the wickedness of the system that would sentence a mere child to death for a belief, young Ibaragi cried again, "Where is my cross?" Directed to the smallest cross on the hill, he ran and embraced it as a child holds on to its most prized possession. During all their sufferings, Louis was an inspiration to all the rest because of his joyous constancy.

"Louis," said Kenny, "and thirteen-year-old Anthony, of Chinese and Japanese parentage, started what would become a characteristic of the Kirishitan Holocaust. They began to sing, 'Praise the Lord ye children, praise the Name of the Lord.' Barely had they finished singing when the spears entered their bodies and darkness fell upon Japan."

Two hundred and fifty years and a world war later, the stage was now set for this Christian spirit to be revived, not only in Kyoto, where it once had been, but all over Japan as American Missionaries were challenged to come to Japan with their message of hope and love for a people who had been humbled by the ravages of a world war.

# Chapter 3

# *Kenny Joseph's Long and Winding Road to Japan*

Kenneth Robert Joseph describes his family as "boat people from Iraq." Although he and his siblings were born in Chicago, his parents, Martha and Sam Joseph, had fled what they called the great Assyrian Holocaust in 1917, when Kurdish and Turkish Muslims were said to have massacred more than 780,000 Assyrian and a million and a half Armenian Christians.

"On Easter, in 1917, the Muslims broke into an evening worship service and asked the Assyrian Christians if they believed in the resurrection," Joseph said, recalling stories he was told as a child by his parents. "If the Assyrians denied the resurrection and embraced the Koran – they could live. If they chose Christianity, they would die by the sword. That night all the local elders told the young, 'run in the snow over the mountains for three days. Get to Christian Russia or Iran. Take a left turn to London and then take a boat to Chicago. Your relatives are waiting there.'"

Born in Nineveh, Iraq, Samuel Noah Joseph was among those that ran in thick wool socks and eventually arrived in Chicago with eight dollars in his pocket. Martha Moshe Adams, another Assyrian immigrant, had also settled in the burgeoning Assyrian community in Chicago. Mentored by Presbyterian missionaries in a seminary in Iran, she came to Chicago with the goal of being a missionary serving in a foreign land. But her Assyrian pastor, Rev. Haidew Ablahat, ordered her to settle down with one of three eligible Assyrian men. She chose Sam Joseph. Together they would have five children. Although they endured the tragic death of their eldest son, six-year-old John, who drowned in the Chicago River, they were later blessed with four more children, including Kenneth Robert Joseph or Kenny, born on October 30th, 1928 on the north side of Chicago in an ethnically diverse neighborhood, Albany Park. This neighborhood included the Marcy's who were Roman Catholics to their left, and a Jewish family, the Schwartz's, to their right, and the agnostic Kimmel family behind them. However, the Josephs wanted to fit in with mainstream American culture in naming their children John, Mildred, Jeanne, Barbara, and Kenny. "Since they were Assyrians now in the USA," recalled Kenny, "they wanted us to have pure USA names, not strange Assyrian names like Sennacarib or Nebuchadnezzer."

Sam Joseph worked three different jobs in the real estate and hotel business to provide for his family often, not coming home until 2 a.m. He didn't like the idea of paying rent – when he could own a house – so he decided to have one built for $16,000. The house had a concrete basement, a first floor, and an attic. It was a six-room house heated by a single coal-fed furnace. "Living in Chicago felt as cold as Alaska," remembered Kenny. "There were freezing winters and hot summers, so we all bundled up in the winter with mufflers and overcoats. School was never cancelled for snow, even though students like me had to walk eight blocks to get there." He remembers shoveling snow around the door, the stairs, and the sidewalk. Finances were rough, and Kenny and his sisters got odd jobs for spending money. "The Big joke in our family was we'd sneak into Dad's bedroom where he slept from 2 a.m. on. We'd go to his pants pocket hanging up and pull out loose change to spend that day." However, Sam Joseph "worked like a dog" and saved up to help all four kids go to college later.

Martha Adams Joseph worked full-time raising her children. "She chased me around the dining room table with a wooden spoon to punish me for something I did wrong," said Kenny. "No washer, dryer, microwave, TV, fridge or fax... Our favorite from Mother's cooking was her dolma made from grape leaves around rice, lamb and spices... I was made to go with the mothers to pick grape leaves in dangerous places. I was the rattle-snake watcher to warn them to run if I heard or saw one." They would have Uncle Shaby and Uncle Elia over for chicken and rice on dolma. They did not have TV back then, so instead, Uncle Shaby would entertain them with stories.

Living with three sisters had its ups and downs and he sometimes got into arguments with them. "I felt we were all treated the same," recalled Kenny, "but the three girls felt I was favored, being the only boy. I know I was spanked the most and never had enough to eat because of my sisters watching."

Kenny recalls his first vivid memory of prayer. "I remember my first day at school," wrote Kenny. "Mom walked me the eight blocks to Volta

Elementary School. She said, 'At 3:30 you walk out that door and walk straight to Central Park, turn left, and you're home.' Being left-handed and direction-dumb, I walked out the opposite door and walked eight blocks away from home. Nothing looked familiar. Then, in the middle of the sidewalk, a big black mountain of black coal appeared. (They put the coal in the basement window.) My little brain said, This is the end of the world. If I go over that I'll drop off the edge of the earth! I prayed kneeling down. Some kids playing ball in the street asked, 'What's the matter?' I said, 'I'm lost!' 'Where do you live?' they inquired 'In a brown brick house near the Chicago River.' 'The street?' 'Central Park.' 'That's a mile that way, get on the back of my bike and I'll take you there.'" So he got home.

A later school experience was much more traumatic: the near-death of his best friend. "At grammar school one day on [the] way to school," he remembered, "a car plowed into a bunch of us kids. It missed me, but my best buddy, John Jergens, was under the tire, and I saw blood coming out of his eye." John survived, and Kenny knew he was also spared for a reason.

Young Kenny enjoyed trips out of the city as a child. "I loved going to Uncle Abe's farm in Knox, Indiana, every summer as soon as school was out in Chicago. There we had a little one-room cottage... Dad stayed in Chicago to work at two jobs after shipping us all, Mom, Mill, Joanne, and me to Knox, driving or taking the train. It was a big deal to get all of us on the Nickle Plate railroad from La Salle St. Station to Knox, 90 miles – two to three hours. The big, mean conductor with his round black hat scared me. At Knox, we had two friends, Phil George and Norm Keena. We called ourselves the Three Musketeers... One day on the farm in Knox, we three boys... climbed up the hayloft in Uncle Abe's barn. As we were playing in the hay, I saw a huge purple-black spider. Sure that he got on my back, I ran to the second floor window and jumped out to lay on the hay on the ground. To kill the spider I rolled and rolled on the ground hoping I'd squash it. Meanwhile the old dog Shep noticed and came running to bite my legs to stop it. I still hate spiders."

Life in the summer was not all idyllic. "While on the farm in Knox," he recalled, "Uncle Abe's wife Abigail went to the Mayo Clinic with cancer. I was in the bathtub when word came that Auntie died. At the funeral I was too short to see the coffin. Norm coldly said, 'No use crying over spilled milk.'"

Something that happened there in the country made him feel that God had a special calling on his life. "I was about seven and on the farm," he remembered. "Ran in the wet grass in [the morning] and picked eggs in the henhouse with a lot of dust from feathers. That night I had severe asthma and was really almost dying. Mom got so scared, she called for Rev. Sleman who lived the next farm away. It took an hour for him to come. He came at midnight to pray for my healing. He prayed and I didn't die. I knew God spared me for a purpose, yet I was not saved."

Since his mother went to a Presbyterian Seminary after they crossed over the border into Tehran, she felt obligated to take her children to the nearest Presbyterian Church. They also went occasionally to Carter Memorial Church, the only Assyrian church in the city, named after a famous missionary.

"Mom dragged me to Sunday school for fifteen straight years without missing a Sunday, sick or well, rain or snow, and I have the Sunday school pins to prove it," Kenny remembered. "Dad got home at 2 a.m. and snored until noon on Sunday."

When he was five years old, Kenny was baptized, wearing a new sailor suit and a whistle for the ceremony, and upon being "sprinkled" with water on his head, shouted, "Mommy, he's getting my suit all wet and promptly blew his whistle! So much for a serious ceremony."

"I never missed one Sunday School," Kenny remembered. "But I wasn't born again; I was a good, hell bound, lost– Presbyterian. The Pastor was the type who said, 'Everyday in every way we are getting better and better.' And so I thought I was a Christian: I was... the Chairman of the Youth Committee, sang in the Choir, [and] played on the Church basketball team."

Not everything in church went over his head. Kenny remembers "Mr. McCain, my Sunday School teacher who made me memorize... 'Create in me a clean heart and put a right spirit in me, O Lord.' Even though I was unsaved, he made me repeat that every night before sleep. Also he came out to my high school baseball games to coach me and cheer."

Despite his status as a baptized, churchgoing young man, Kenny would later describe himself as an "unsaved hell-bound leader of the Albany Park Presbyterian Church youth group."

"We met in Pastor Michael's basement and had necking parties until he would come down to check. Our scout whistled and then we started singing hymns. He walked back up to tell his wife how impressed he was with this wonderful bunch," he recalled.

As if that wasn't bad enough, Kenny joined a street gang while attending Von Steuben High School. The gang was called The Stigers, derived from the terms "stinkers" and "tigers."

"We were the toughest gang in the school, and we were respected," said Kenny. "The leader of the gang was Art Meridian, a tough Armenian. He led us into fights with Jews, Italians, Swedes, and other minorities. We did a lot of stupid pranks but only once got into minor trouble with the law. My mother would have died had she known what we were up to, but she prayed me through those troubled years and made me memorize Bible verses for a dime each."

"Back in 1945," he went on, "there were no guns in the gang warfare, just brass knuckles. I had a BB gun, and one day a gang buddy, John Jergens, and I shot a girl with it. It went through her fur coat and she started to cry. We were sure she would call the police, so we went and hid in neighbor McPherson's basement and watched out the window, but the police never came."

One time he won five dollars for eating seventeen live goldfish at one time. Another time, he won five dollars for going to high school all throughout the cold winter with his shirt sleeves rolled up.

When Kenny was in high school, he loved baseball – and he lived in the perfect city. "I went to ball games whenever I could find an excuse to go to Eugene Field close by home or to River Park in high school to play softball or real baseball," he recalled. "But the best was to go see the Chicago Cubs at Wrigley Field one hour away from home by street car. But you had to pay to get in. So I decided to get a job selling peanuts, popcorn, etc. in Cubs Park. I could see all the games for nothing and make spending money at the same time."

Kenny recalls that his biggest heroes were Joe DiMaggio and members of the U.S. Navy.

"I wanted to join the Navy and be a better baseball player than 'Joltin' Joe,'" he said. "I wasn't tall or heavy enough, so I hung from the tree in front of our house and ate bananas to put on weight and get tall enough. That obviously didn't work. How could I become better than Joe DiMaggio? Practice six hours a day, even with my baseball suit under my school clothes and my bat and glove beside me on the piano bench as I practiced music. And then, like Superman, I'd shed my school clothes and play baseball until dark. Getting better, yet not good enough."

Young Kenny got Joe's autograph three times and on one occasion told his hero, "Joe, I plan to take your job. How can I get better than you?"

DiMaggio answered with one word: "Hah!" and patted Kenny's head.

"On the way home, I thought: If I could somehow get Joe DiMaggio's spirit inside of me, then when I play center field like he does, I'll have his spirit and his power. And I could be the best fielder and hit the most home runs," Kenny remembered. "Well, after my successful high school baseball career, we had tryouts for the Major Leagues and I won a spot. We went to Wrigley Field to play against the Cubs. Since I had worked at and watched 77 games while selling popcorn, I was sure I knew my way around, and thought, 'piece of cake.'

"But when I got to the batter's box and saw the pitcher, he looked nine feet tall, and the mound was at least four feet high! I looked and felt like a dwarf. Then I prayed (even though I wasn't a born-again Christian): 'May the spirit of Joe DiMaggio come into me.' I added two verses from Psalms: 'Trust in the Lord with all your heart and lean not on your own understanding. In all your ways acknowledge Him and He will direct your paths,' and 'Delight thyself also in the Lord and He will give you the desires of your heart.' The desire of my heart right then was to hit a home run. So I went up there trying to bat against these pitchers, and it looked like there was a mountain up there... 'Dear Jesus my desire is to hit a home run, Amen.' 'Strike One.' 'You said that verse about delighting Lord, and I'm delighting!' 'Strike two.' 'Lord don't let me down here, I've only got one left and I'm going to hit a homerun and become a Chicago Cub,' and I hit line drive to the catcher...

"Strike three, you're out!" was the umpire's answer to his prayer.

"Joe, where were you when I needed you?" Kenny said under his breath.

"So much for the spirit of Joe DiMaggio coming into me!" he said. "And, so much for my baseball career. A lot of prayer, but no power. Why? Because I wasn't plugged into the power source. A car with no battery: pretty on the outside, nothing inside. I wonder if I had become a Chicago Cubs player what would I be now?"

Kenny had another hobby – playing piano – which was not his choice at the time. However, he would be thankful for it later. "I was made to take lessons, dragged, kicking and screaming," he wrote. "I'd put my baseball uniform on under my clothes so as soon as mt teacher was done I could play baseball, not piano. I had a hard time reading notes and playing. Then when boogie-woogie became popular, I went to a specialist who, in a few weeks' time, taught me how to play any song in C on three flats by chords. Even to this day I can play almost any song in those two keys if I hear the melody. Wasn't God good since after coming to Japan, I had to play the accordion with chords. In my evangelistic travels I'd play any song requested by heart."

In the meantime, Kenny's mother persisted in her belief that God had a divine plan for her son, and gang-banging or professional baseball weren't part of it. She wanted him to be a missionary, to do the work that she had hoped to do, but was unable to. Well aware of her son's downward spiral, she did the only thing she knew to be effective: She prayed.

"I could take you to Mother's bedroom where there were two holes in the rug made by her knees where she prayed for her prodigal son," Kenny recalled.

Eventually, there was a turning point for her rebellious teenager. In high school chemistry class, Kenny sat next to Marian Anderson, a missionary daughter and a girl who he knew to be a "goody-goody" girl who attended Christian youth clubs. Marian told him about a particularly large rally that was being held in the 78,000 seat Soldier's Field. What Kenny didn't know was that his mother Martha had spent the previous year praying, along with a thousand other mothers, that the crusade would be successful and that it wouldn't rain.

"In Chemistry class, my girlfriend said, 'There is a YFC big stadium rally in Soldier's Field, on May 30th,'" remembered Kenny. "My mother and a thousand other women in Chicago were praying for a whole year, 'Dear God, have it not rain on May 30th, Memorial Day, we are going to have a huge YFC crusade.' 'Big deal Mom [I thought]', just call the weatherman and ask him what the weather's going to be on May 30th, you don't have to pray for it, don't have to waste God's time to get it."

"I was downtown with my high school gang. We didn't have enough money to go to the South side Chicago burlesque show," Kenny recalled. "Suddenly we saw a tall man with arms stretched out wider than an eagle's telling people to go to Soldier's Field. He quoted one of the verses that my mother had made me memorize for 10 cents, 'For all have sinned and come short of the glory of God.' We derisively walked away, but since the youth rally was free and Gil Dodds, Olympic champion, was going to run an exhibition mile race, I said, 'Why not?' and walked into the stadium. They said this was a youth Olympic rally, but there was a choir of three hundred nurses singing Christian songs. Then it all came back. This was what Marian was talking about. And it was what my mother were praying about. A young man named Billy Graham gave a three-minute testimony. Then Charles E. Fuller, the famous evangelist of radio's 'Old Fashioned Revival Hour,' preached."

Kenny rebelliously prayed, "God, if there is a God, send rain so I can go home and bug mom for wasting a whole year praying for this."

"It suddenly started to rain and Fuller said, 'Put down your umbrellas. Let's believe God to stop the rain. Let's pray.' And the rain stopped... in front of 78,000 people. I thought, 'I don't know what that man has or how to get it, but I want it.' I had never been in an invitation setting before, but after his message he gave one for everyone to come down and kneel at the 200-foot long white wooden cross on the football field. He led us in the Sinner's Prayer. As I was praying, a personal worker came and put her arm around my shoulder. Her voice sounded familiar, and I looked up into the face of my dear Mother who had prayed seventeen years for this. The verse in II Cor. 5:17 became true as we hugged each other—'therefore if any man be in Christ he is a new creature, old things pass away and all things become new.'"

Fellow gang members were skeptical that Kenny's transformation would last. Kenny recalls one of his high school friends saying, "Give him 12 days and he will be back."

Kenny, however, was sincere. Later, he spoke at a Youth For Christ rally at the Chicago Orchestra Hall where Bob Cook, the YFC president, introduced him after George Beverly Shea sang. As he was giving his testimony, Shea pulled on his coat and said, "A testimony, not a sermon." Kenny realized that he needed training if he was going to grow in his newfound faith and he saw an ad on the back of Moody Monthly magazine for "the world's most unusual university – Bob Jones University." So in the fall of 1946, he boarded a train to Cleveland, Tennessee, where the school was located at the time and enrolled.

"At Bob Jones, there were a thousand male students in the 'Preacher Boys Class' and the director of extension, Dr. Stenholm, was promoting YFC and TEAM Mission," Kenny recalled. "On one vacation period, I went to Chicago and interviewed to be a TEAM missionary on loan to YFC and I was accepted.

"On the way to Bob Jones University, I met a young fellow on the train and I led him to the Lord. I said, 'Where are you from?' And he said, 'North Carolina.' And I said, 'I'm going to come and see you sometime.' I had no idea how far away he was. But we got to Bob Jones University, and would you believe, he was just forty miles away. One of our first ideas was to go and meet this young fellow, and instead of meeting him, I met this old lady who was saved at a Billy Sunday meeting and had a little shop there which played Christian music."

She told Kenny, "We need something for the young people here. They're going to hell, and we need something to help them."

So, although he never met the young man again, he heeded the request of this lady and in 1948, began a Youth For Christ rally every Friday night. After school, he would drive the 40 miles from Bob Jones University in Greenville, SC to Hendersonville, NC. He became the YFC director there for five years as well as being a full-time student. His weekends were filled with evangelistic meetings, and soon he had set up thirteen YFC rallies in cities like Greenville, Athens, Atlanta, Charlotte, and Hendersonville.

"We had about thirteen student groups going out every weekend," recalled Kenny. "We had no insurance, no money, and no salary. We just went there and took an offering in YFC baskets to help cover our expenses, but we never had any guarantee of anything."

Kenny recalled that while he was running the Hendersonville rallies, there was a local Methodist pastor who he described as "a very liberal, modernistic, Methodist pastor who didn't like anything about us. But we got people saved, born again and back into the church and he couldn't believe what was happening to the people. He told me one day, 'These were the people who were baptized in my Church. What's going on here?' And he finally came over to our side, because we produced something for him. There was also Faith Tabernacle, a little old church out of town, and there, YFC brought hundreds, and that little church started their own radio program, and those young people just multiplied many times."

Kenny said that soon he was able to start a local YFC radio program in which they told listeners that those who came to Christ should "go back to a Bible-believing church of your choice."

During his junior year at Bob Jones, Kenny expressed his new commitment to serving the Lord as he was baptized again. "I was re-baptized by Rev. Hester and ordained at the Hendersonville, NC, Baptist Church at 21 years old where I was director of Youth for Christ."

"I was under the stars, the big beautiful place where there were no trees, let alone buildings, and it was as the Psalmist said, "When I consider the heavens, the stars and the work of your hands, what is man that

Thou art mindful of him? The son of man that Thou visitest him? Made him a little lower than the angels." That great, great God of the universe, which is unimaginably big–He runs the whole thing. And we think we are the center of God's universe and we're a little piece of sand. And yet He's got the whole world in His hand. And He's got you and me. And He's got everything else under control.'

I was at Bob Jones selling shoes. Clean new shoes to dirty, smelly feet. I knew there was something more that God had for me, but I stuttered and I couldn't preach. So I knew I would never preach. That was just taken for granted. If I could just get through answering a question, that was a big deal. You remember how I went to a street meeting and got healed of stuttering and I won my first soul, a black man and put my arm around him kneeling there, and some white guy came up and said, "Hey, you n---- lovers from Bob Jones, what are you doing, hugging him down there?"

But I still wasn't called to preach. I knew I couldn't preach. And a man named Ray Cutchins was selling *Sword of the Lord* books and he tried to sell me some and he had his card, and he said, 'Hey, have you ever surrendered to preach?' 'What does that mean?' I wondered. And he took me in his car – in the front seat and we were talking and he said, 'Have you ever told God that you would quit fighting the call to preach and if He called you to preach, you'd say yes?' Now remember there are two kinds of calls. One says GPC. This guy said 'I was a farmer plowing my field and I saw this big sign and it said, 'G PC.' 'Wow! A sign from heaven.' I knew that meant Go preach Christ. And yet the guy couldn't preach. He tried to preach somewhere and made a food of himself. He just couldn't preach. He couldn't talk in public. The more he tried, the worse it was. Then an old fellow asked him about the GPC. 'What was that now?' 'Yeah, God gave me a sign, GPC. Go Preach Christ.' His friend replied: 'Are you sure it didn't mean Go Plant Corn?' So this guy said to me. 'Don't try to push God, but if He's called you to preach, you'll know it. And He'll show it to you.' So, I surrendered to preach. That's a term they use down South. I said, 'OK God, you're the greatest God, you're the biggest God. You know everything. And I'm not arrogant to tell you what I'm going to do for you. I'll do whatever you want me to do.' So then I was praying as most students do in the morning with my little prayer list which I started in 1946 and I seemed to hear a little voice saying, 'Isaiah 61:1' And I didn't know if there were that many chapters in the book of Isaiah, but I said, 'OK, I'll try.' I just tried to put it out of my mind, but it kept coming back. I had never read it. So I looked, and there I read what is also in Luke 4:18. 'The Spirit of the Lord is upon me and He has anointed me to preach Good Tidings, Good news. He has anointed me to preach.' And that was my call to preach and I never have changed it."

Soon, a series of mini revivals were taking place all over the region, led by this former rebel Kenny Joseph. As things progressed, he felt he needed a new challenge. He read about General Douglas McArthur's call for 5000 missionaries and 10 million New Testaments to come to Japan in the YFC magazine.

The article asked, "Who will come and help these poor Japanese just after the war? They have no food, and there is a spiritual vacuum." He read that the Emperor had devastated his people by renouncing his divinity.

Shortly after this, Kenny attended a week-long YFC conference at Winona Lake, Indiana, near Chicago. During the conference Kenny met Eddie Reece, a Moody Bible Institute graduate. The speakers included Bob Pierce, who showed a movie about Asia, and Louie Zamporine, who gave a testimony of how he was captured by the Japanese and was saved in a P.O.W. camp.

One of the speakers gave a challenge for missionaries to go to Japan, saying, "This open door is not only open; it's been broken off its hinges. Who will come?"

Kenny turned to Eddie and said, "Let's go forward, and let's just say to God that we're willing to be missionaries, but don't you dare send us."

Kenny's rationale was that if God saw that they were willing, he would say, "Okay, you don't have to go."

But it wasn't long before both of them realized that God's call on their lives to go to Japan was for real, and they both made the decision that they would go!

"At Christmas, when Eddie and I were both 22, instead of going to snowy Chicago, I went to New Smyrna Beach, Florida, to pray," recalled Kenny. "I asked the Lord to show us if He wanted Eddie and me to go to Japan as a Gospel team. I said I was willing, and if we got meetings between where we were and Japan, we would go."

Two days later a telegram came from Montana Youth For Christ director Franklin Robbie saying, 'can book you 22 straight nights at YFC rallies. Reply by wire.'"

Kenny called Eddie in Grand Rapids, Michigan, and said, "Let's go!"

Eddie and Kenny pooled their funds and bought an old Chevy for ninety-eight dollars and headed through snowstorms and buffaloes for their first meeting in Conrad, Montana. When they arrived they had eighteen cents left, enough for one gallon of gas.

"The first night after we sang and preached and testified, many came forward for salvation and consecration for missions. The offering plate had thirty-three silver dollars, and we ran to the bank the next day and exchanged those for 'real' money," Kenny remembered. Now they're worth ninety dollars each.

Soon, Kenny and Eddie were on their way to Japan and a new life in a country that had been devastated by war.

"I bought a wardrobe locker with drawers, hangers for clothes – everything I needed to live," he remembered. "Being warned that Japan had no food, we bought all the canned food we could handle and were allowed, which was 350 pounds each, plus whatever we could stuff into our state room on this twelve-passenger freighter going to Japan. We left from the Home of Peace in Oakland, California."

"We had to get on the ship on April 14$^{th}$, 1951, and Eddie's passport hadn't come yet, but he got on anyway. Halfway across the ocean the captain learned that Eddie had no passport. Enraged, he said, 'President Truman himself couldn't land without a passport. You are going directly to jail.' Eddie prayed a lot!"

When they arrived in Yokohama, TEAM Misson's Karl Notehelfer came on board to deliver Eddie's passport. Dr. Clyde Taylor, President of the NAE, Washington, had mailed it to the TEAM office in Tokyo.

For Kenny, the trip would prove to be educational. "Today, there are many seminars and books on the 'mystique of the Japanese people and their country,' but I learned all about that during fourteen days on the American President Line's ship, the Wilson sailing from San Francisco to Yokohama from April 14$^{th}$ to 28$^{th}$, 1951... On board were twelve passengers who ate three meals in formal fashion at the captain's table," he recalled.

Kenny recalled, "My tutor was Kiyoshi Togasaki, a Christian businessman and owner-publisher of the Nippon Times, the patriotic wartime name for the Japan Times of today. After we all introduced ourselves, the stately Mr. Togasaki learned that my parents were from the city of Nineveh, now Mosul, In Iraq, where Jonah went to preach God's Judgment ('repent or be destroyed in 40 days!') upon the Assyrians. The king repented and made every living thing, human and animal, fast and pray for 40 days to avert God's impending judgment. It worked. To this day the Assyrians call themselves the 'only Christian nation in the world.'"

Kenny said that when he mentioned his Assyrian heritage, Togasaki replied, "Persians, Assyrians, Nestorians? Your people brought over to us three priceless treasures: the Bible's Gospel, democracy, and medicine."

And, after telling him some of Japan's history that is not written in books, Togasaki said, "Japanese history is fairy tales, 'his story' vs. 'my story.' You must become a lifelong student of true history and a proponent of this magnificent unwritten Christian testimony." Re. Toyohiko Kagawa said, "Japan's history is a tissue of lies."

In the course of eating and being aboard the ship with him for two weeks, Kenny said that he learned what a true, upright Japanese was. Togasaki told the gripping story of how he, as an important businessman, lost everything in the tragic San Francisco earthquake of 1928.

"Because all records were burned, there was an amnesty that [said] 'you didn't have to pay anything you couldn't find the bill for' but he proudly declared, 'I'm a Japanese Christian! I got in my horse-drawn buggy and went to every single company or person I owed money to. We wrote from memory all the bills and I paid every last penny. How could I do anything else before an all-seeing, all-knowing God?'"

Then he showed Kenny pictures of him as an evangelist preaching to thousands of people before and after World War II. He would hand-print huge song sheets one by one, and after leading the singing, would preach the Gospel. His favorite message was, "Jesus said, 'I am the way, the truth and the life; No one comes to the Father except through me.'"

"To understand how the deep significance of my meeting Mr. Togasaki was, is to understand the background from which I came," said Kenny. "My father and mother escaped a holocaust... and I grew up hearing horror stories of Moslem massacres from cousins and family friends. When I told my parents that God had called me to Japan, my Dad fumed. 'You're crazy! Those Japanese men walk around in kimonos with two swords, one big and one small. If they get mad, they'll kill you. Don't go near that place!' So when I met this stately, Godly gentleman – instead of what I had feared – I was overwhelmed. We led two joint Sunday morning services aboard the ship. He led the singing and I preached. He also took the offering and dedicated it to my future work in Japan. That was the first offering I had ever received from a Japanese hand. And that's how I've lived by faith for all these years, from God's hand to my mouth.

From Togasaki Kenny says he learned these ten principles:

* Punctuality ("jikan genshu")
* Neatness ("kichin toshite")
* Frugality ("setsuyaku")
* Integrity ("shinyo")
* Knowing and repaying obligations ("giri-ninjo" and "on")
* Filial piety ("oyakoko")
* Respect for elders ("sempai sonkei")
* Tighten your belt and keep going ("gambare")
* Honesty ("shojiki")
* Reality and phony spirituality ("honne" and "tatemae")

"He didn't have to parade it, it showed in the sparkle in his eyes," said Kenny of his first Japanese friend. "He was a man at peace with himself and God. Those ten lessons – as well as a lot of other lessons learned from Togasaki – helped me with all of the ups and downs, victories and defeats, pluses and minuses, merits and demerits of living, working, loving, suffering and surviving in Japan since 1951. Why? Because I learned that is what a born-again Japanese Christian believer can become. Although every day we read about and see on TV scandals in every section of society – politicians, bankers, doctors, real estate agents, businessmen, school presidents, public servants, teachers, professors…that is merely looking at Japan with the naked eye. Put on 'Bible's binoculars' and see past the outward to what the inner can become, and you have millions of miracles of Christians in Japan. When there are more like him, there'll be more Christians. There's a saying that to tell if a stick is crooked, you put it alongside a straight one. Togasaki was a 'straight stick.'"

"The Cold War also brought a new wave of missionaries to Japan that changed the makeup of Japan's foreign Christian community," noted author Tim Shorrock. "Many of the new arrivals were fundamentalist and rigidly anti-communist and soon outnumbered the liberals by nearly four to one. Many of them had arrived in Japan after fleeing communist-controlled areas in China and Korea. Others were recruited from American denominations founded during the Cold War atmosphere of the late 1940s and early 1950s to counter the liberal bias of the mainstream Disciples, Methodists and Presbyterians. Upon their arrival in Japan, they were shocked by the involvement of Christians in the opposition to the Korean War and the tolerant attitude of many Christians towards communism and Marxism."

"I thought I could come for a one-year Youth for Christ gospel team, just actually living in holes, people carved in ashes," Kenny remembered. "Wherever we go we'd have a crowd. Well, God never ordains a great seed sowing unless He has in His mind a great harvest. That kept us going, we had a reaping time when other missionaries and pastors had sowed, and we were going there and cutting the grain. God sent a revival. TEAM's policy was 'language study first.' YFC's policy was 'evangelize...forget the language. Jesus is coming back soon.' President Eisenhower predicted a worldwide atomic war with the world ending in 1952. 'Who needs the language?' we thought. At our first YFC meeting in Tokyo in front of 800 people at Shibuya train Station, I gave my testimony and it started to rain. Again we prayed and it stopped. 108 people came forward to kneel in the dirt and accept Christ. There was a great temptation to begin evangelizing right then."

But Kenny reluctantly followed orders, making the 100 mile trek up the mountains to quiet Karuizawa, where he went to 'Yale Jail,' the nickname for the Yale Language School. The average family with two children would take two years in language study. However, Kenny, as a bachelor, went through the program in eight months. He learned how to preach one sermon in Japanese: "God, Sin and Salvation."

Regarding Japanese food in those early days, Kenny observed, "The only food resembling American was rice wrapped in a scrambled egg, or pork on top of rice. They didn't know hamburger from a steak, but you could buy a bowl of hot noodles from a portable roadside stand for 15 cents. I quickly learned not to eat raw fish. My next door neighbor's eight-year-old boy died of food poisoning after eating it."

Every weekend during language study, Kenny would go out with Gospel tracts. Whenever they stopped, a crowd would quickly form, and they would be surrounded by outstretched hands wanting the tracts.

""It rained all night and morning so our plans to go to a new mountain city were overruled," Kenny wrote in his journal on a typical day, Sunday June 19$^{th}$, 1951. "We cancelled all plans to go out, but after noon, the sun cleared all up, so we went out to two new, untouched villages 13 miles south. We took the newest teacher, Matsumoto-san. First stop was a vast pack of rice paddies with 75 different farmers each tending their own handkerchief size plot. Don played Japanese records while we walked about one and a half mils giving out Gospel tracts. Then we drove to the next town where we parked, played some Gospel records while again we two walked into town to pass out literature. Then, as usual, a crowd of children were gathered by the sound truck, so we went to the back, taught them two songs "Rolled Away" and "What a Friend We Have In Jesus." We told them we'd be back then drove to the next town and did the very same thing and we had a better reception, more older folks also. I took some pictures, then drove on back, passing out tracts. After supper we heard drums so Don and I tracked them down and found a regular Shinto service. Don took a time exposure: here was heathenism in the raw like that in Africa. God help us to see the battle."

"While on the first mission station we continued language study and worked with Jerry and Miriam Johnson," he recalled. Every night we held outdoor Gospel meetings with hundreds attending, and everyone getting Gospel tracts. Usually 10% or more would come forward to get saved."

Kenny then bought a British Austin pick-up truck, put his steamer trunk in it, and left language school for a village in Shizoka to live with TEAM missionaries Jim and Ruth Frens.

"Since there was no Christian language book or manual to go by, I began making illustrations to be used in messages for myself every day."

"Today I have been in Japan one year and have seen at least 1,300 sincere Japanese profess faith in Jesus Christ," Kenny noted in his journal on May 1st, 1952. "With many doubts, fears, anxieties and cares I rededicated my life to win souls to Jesus. I packed, took care of final details and shoved off from Shizuoka."

But Kenny's newfound work in Japan was nearly cut short, however, when he was diagnosed with tuberculosis:

"After preaching for seven straight months on the road from my pick-up truck... my body's immune system was so low that if I got a scratch it wouldn't heal," he recalled. "TB germs were everywhere, even in the dust from driving on gravel roads. I was feeling tired, beat, exhausted. A complete checkup at Niigata Hospital showed TB in the left lung. The doctor ordered, 'Six months complete bed rest.'"

Kenny's bout with tuberculosis caused him to slow down but after a long recovery, a wiser Kenny Joseph took better care of himself and prepared for the jouney ahead.

For Kenny Joseph, another great adventure was about to begin.

## Chapter 4

# *Lila from the Prairie*

"Er du rusukute, Bestefar?" ("Are you out of your mind, Grandpa?") was Lila May Finsaas' shocked response when, as a little girl who wouldn't go to bed, she stood halfway up the stairway and noticed that her grandfather, at the bottom of the stairway, was holding a spanking stick behind his back! She was later assured that this was a very clever statement – for a four-year-old!

"Until the age of seven, I heard Norwegian spoken constantly from family and friends," Lila remembered, "from family and friends. Then we moved into a predominantly German community and Norwegian was put on the back burner of my mind."

While Kenny's heritage was Assyrian from the Nineveh Plains of Iraq, the legacy that Lila inherited couldn't have been more different. Her grandparents on both sides as well as her mother came from the Kingdom of Norway, a constitutional monarchy in northern Europe that occupies the western portion of the Scandinavian Peninsula.

"It's a great heritage, this Norwegian-American Experience," Lila said. "Two of the best combinations and I'm proud of both. Thanks to my Mom and Dad!"

Lila was born and spent the first seven years of her life close to the city of Schafer in North Dakota.

"My Dad homesteaded there, and in the earlier years it was a booming Midwest town, but then the railroad came through and bypassed Schafer, going to Watford City," she recalled, "so Schafer became a ghost town, which is how I remember it."

Her father's parents emigrated from Norway and settled in Iowa. Her grandfather became well-to-do by working in the lumber business.

"My brother Clarence remembers our Grandpa coming home in his horse drawn carriage wearing white gloves, and hired helpers unhitching the horses and taking them to their barns," she recalled. "He was also a lay preacher, and the story goes that once some men knelt in the road in front of his house in mockery of him. But not long afterwards, one of them lost a child, and he asked Grandpa to officiate at the funeral. Mother's family also emigrated from Norway, where Mother was born. She was eight years old when they left their homeland and immigrated to America, landing in Nova Scotia, Canada, and then traveling by train to Iowa where they had relatives. In a short time they also felt the pull to the West, and Grandpa Aarhus went on ahead to Schafer, where he homesteaded, and then Grandma and the rest of the family joined him."

When Lila's mother was seventeen, she got a job in a hotel in Schafer.

"I remember her saying that she had to have three pies baked by breakfast," remembered Lila. "Mother was an unusually good cook, and she never just threw things together. I had never seen eggs scrambled with a fork in the frying pan until I was away from home. Mother always whipped up the eggs and then put them in a covered pan over the flame, and they turned out fluffy and tasty. During this time she and Dad met. Actually, I think both were with other friends when Dad changed places in the car so he could be near Mom. Eventually they were married in a ceremony at her parents' place and began their own life together in humble surroundings. I never thought Dad was sorry he had left so much behind in Iowa. He loved the West all his life. He was a great storyteller, and I remember him joking about a couple that came from Iowa to visit. The wife looked over the vast plains and exclaimed, 'I'd have to love my husband an awful lot to live here!'"

Lila's mother faced the challenge of raising nine children before mass industrialization.

"Many times I wonder how Mother ever managed to keep nine children from serious illness, injury or even death," Lila recalled. "It must have taken constant watchfulness, been a tremendous strain, required a lot of praying and many times seemed a thankless job. I wonder how she kept everybody clothed in a day when she had to make most everything that was worn, and sewn by hand at that. And the washing on the scrubboard. And so many overalls. I know how dirty boys can get, how they go through the knees, and catch their shirts and pants on nails and boards. I wonder how Mom kept us all fed. She couldn't go to the corner supermarket and load up her basket as we do nowadays. Even I can order Japanese noodles and we can slurp them up when I'm in a hurry. Without refrigeration food had to be thought of months in advance. Vegetables and fruits canned by the hundreds of quarts while they were in season... I wonder how she could diagnose and treat illnesses like a doctor. She couldn't pick up her telephone and tell her pediatrician about the sore throat, the fever or the breaking out. I wonder how many dishes Mom washed in her lifetime; how many loaves of bread she baked; how many cakes and pies she made. How many batches of delicious donuts and cookies she made. There were no cake mixes, instant frosting mixes or donut makers, either."

Lila grew up with only one set of grandparents, her mother's parents who lived nearby, while her Dad's parents were in Iowa.

"That was like a far-away country in those days," she said. "His mom died when I was maybe four or five and I remember that when he was gone for her funeral, I cried because I missed him. We often went to Watford to visit Grama and Grampa. Uncle Ted lived with them, and he and Grampa ran the gas station which was next door on the corner. Grampa was responsible for a church being built nearby... Grampa prayed with his hands clasped on the table in front of him with his eyes open. He prayed like this both before and after meals. Grama was a petite lady like a little Japanese grandmother, I've thought. Though she had gone through much heartache in her early married years – losing four children one by one through sickness – she was a cheerful lady who loved to talk. It was all in Norwegian, which she spoke even to my girlfriend Jean who didn't understand a word of it! In the summer our uncles and their families came home to Grama and Grampa's for a couple of weeks. When Uncle Henry and Aunt Helen came from Portland, Jean and I each got a twin to look after, since they brought their boys James and John. The boys must have been six to eight months old. Uncle Henry played the guitar and sang. He was a Wesleyan Methodist minister which must have been quite a change for this Lutheran family. I admired Aunt Helen because she had dark hair and looked French and I thought Uncle Henry was wonderful to marry her. I've thought she was the forerunner to my marrying Kenny, a dark-haired Assyrian!"

When Lila was born, her parents already had seven boys.

Of her addition to the family, Lila said, "Maybe it was like a prize in the midst of the worst depression America had ever known! Growing up, I never felt it strange that I didn't have sisters, and I didn't feel I was overly spoiled, though I do remember when I didn't get my way, I'd head for a bed and cry. Eventually Dad would come and get me. But I also remember when he stopped doing that, and I had to shape up by myself!"

Lila's earliest memory was when she was two years old. Her brother Marvin lifted her up to see her little sister, Helen Arlene, who had died soon after birth, in her casket.

"I wonder what it would have been like to have a sister," she wondered. "But I always had girlfriends and so I don't ever remember feeling that I had missed something in life."

When Lila was about three years old, her mother became deathly ill.

"While Mom was so sick – they expected anytime to hear of her death – she had a life-changing encounter with the Lord," Lila recalled. "She promised Him that if He would heal her, she would give her life to Him and serve Him, though she knew it would be hard because Dad was very anti-Christian. It seemed like he tried to leave spiritual things behind when he left his family in Iowa. But Mom got well, went home, and from then on became a strong Christian and began praying for her family."

As the only daughter in the family, Lila helped out in the kitchen often and was especially fond of her father. "As a child I helped both at home and at a neighbor's during threshing time," she said. "This was a big yearly fall event and housewives went all out to prepare scrumptuous meals for the working men. Neighbors helped each other, so there was often quite a group. But even as a child, I always realized that my Dad was special. When he came in and joined the men for a meal, the whole place livened up. Dad was full of energy and told stories and talked so that it affected the others in a positive, lighthearted way. When neighbors dropped by or relatives came, Dad would tell story after story and sometimes I wondered if he hadn't missed his calling and shouldn't have been a preacher. He always told the stories exactly as they were, never added or subtracted. Once I remember one of my brothers touting, 'I can tell stories just as good as Dad,' and another brother quickly canceled out that smart-alec statement and the subject was closed! I remember Mom being uneasy, though, when Dad recounted in detail the murder of a whole family in the area by one man. I often heard him tell that true story and he ended it with the same sure belief that 'there are people living yet who had part in the lynching from a bridge of the man who committed the murder.'"

The darker details of Lila's father's stories were few and far between, unlike Lila's fondness for her parents and the persisting influence they had throughout her life. The following poem was written by Lila for her

Mom and Dad and read at their Golden Wedding anniversary party in 1963:

*Go West, young man, go West," they cried, and the challenge touched his heart,*
*Those open spaces beckoned so, that he made plans to depart.*

*But when the family heard it they were filled with great dismay,*
*They tried in vain to change his mind, and keep him home to stay.*

*For from the wild and woolly West weird tales had drifted back,*
*Of evil, violence and grief there surely was no lack.*

*"Why, you're life's not worth a nickel, Killers roam at will, they say,*
*"Freely toting guns and arrows, Someone's shot 'most every day.*

*"You will soon become a caveman if you even find a cave,*
*"Here the corn is tall and handsome, There for meager food you'll slave."*

*But he wouldn't be dissuaded, though he loved his family dear,*
*Dauntless, brave and pioneering... he set out without a fear.*

*To be sure, the West was rugged, Summers hot and winters long,*
*Some gave up and called it evil, Others found themselves more strong.*

*Nature greatly joined the testing, Rain was slight and drought prevailed,*
*Grasshoppers in droves descended, Courage ebbed, but never failed.*

*In the West he lived and loved it, Open skies and wide terrain,*
*Friendly neighbors – not so vicious – brightened life out on the plain.*

*There he met his wife of valor, There his children, nine, were reared,*
*Grew and learned to be resourceful, For they, too, must pioneer.*

*And they learned a lesson early: goals before us to be met,*
*Are ne'er fulfilled by dreamy idlers, And quitters never got there yet!*

*Now this girl he found was pretty and she really caught his eye,*
*The very first time that he saw her, He went home a-flyin' high.*

*"You should see that Aarhus girl, boys; A nicer lookin' there can't be,"*
*And with that old determination, He vowed, "That's the one for me!"*

*And she it was who shared the rigors, Strong in spirit, soul and mind,*
*For prairie life of self-denial, Few today are to be found.*

*Many times I marvel deeply that she kept her nine so well,*
*In an illness she was doctor checking tongue and pulse to tell.*

*Keeping all so healthy, frisky; Vitamins were sure unknown,*
*Canning in the fall the produce, That in spring was always sown.*

*Dishes washed would total truckloads; Home-made bread three times a week,*
*Cakes and cookies, without mixes, for their baker well did speak.*

*Sure her nerves were worn and tattered, What one forgot, eight more thought up;*
*They drove the car into the water, Blew up the stove with a covered up.*

*Two fell in the cellar, scuffling; Hit the churn and spilled the cream,*
*One broke an arm when horseback riding, Another when swinging from a beam.*

*But a Higher Power was sought for; Sought to keep and sought to save*
*from the world's alluring pitfalls, many hours of prayer she gave.*

*From the Bible she claimed verses that the Lord would save them all,*
*Draw them to Himself eternal, Help each one to hear His call.*

*Hear His call to full surrender; Nothing less than all for Him,*
*When the heavenly roll call's taken, All must be there, saved from sin.*

*Now the kids are all grown up and scattered far across the earth,*
*How they all would like to be there on this day to share your mirth.*

*And to say to Mom and Daddy on your Golden Wedding Day,*
*Thanks for all your love and patience as you led us in the Way.*

*Thanks for discipline and firmness, Thanks for lessons old and new,*
*Thanks for tender care and sweetness, Thanks to God Who gave us you!*

When Lila was seven years old, her father decided to move about 50 miles west into the beautiful Yellowstone Valley because that was irrigation country.

"I often felt that Dad went out West to pioneer partly to get away from the Christian influence of his family,' Lila said 'His Dad was a businessman with three sawmills, but also a lay preacher… I thought he was kinda running away from God's call on his life because I went through a time like that during my teen-age years. But Dad made the 'mistake' of marrying into even more of a Christian family – two of Mom's brothers became pastors – and finally when I was three, Mom gave herself fully to the Lord."

The family also had practical reasons for moving.

"He had gone through several years of drought and had had it," Lila said. "So we moved there, but my brother Marvin stayed on so he could finish high school in Watford City. In those early years immigrants settled together in neighborhoods and cities, and up until now we had been in a predominantly Scandinavian community. But in the Fairview area where we moved to, most of the people were German-speaking. The state line runs through Fairview, and we used to say that when you drove through town, you had two wheels in North Dakota and two wheels in Montana. From then on I grew up in North Dakota, but most everything I did was in Montana, so to keep the confusion down, I said I was from Montana. It took a while for us to be welcomed in Fairview. The kids gave Ray a hard time at school and me a hard time on the walk home. A group of us walked home from school about half a mile to our place, and then the rest walked on to their homes further north. Though I didn't tell her, Mother caught on that the kids were teasing me on the way home, and one afternoon she suddenly appeared from behind some bushes, and I think that was the end of that particular problem. As the years went by, the girl who was the ringleader became my good friend, and we went through 8th grade together."

Not long after moving, the family had a surprise addition: Lila's youngest brother Orvin was born when she was nine years old.

"Orvin was a big surprise," she said. "From the very beginning he was sunshine in our home. I sometimes used to think, 'What would we do if we didn't have Orvin?' Everything connected with babies, until they were born, was so secretive in those days. My Grama – Mom's Mom – came to visit, and one day she told me in Norwegian that my Mom was going to have a baby, and then she added, 'Oh, I guess I shouldn't have told you that!' Mom was surprised that even the older brothers enjoyed the new baby so much. We have a picture of him and Clarence when he was about two, with 25 years difference in their ages. Orvin waited for me to come home from school by the bus, and he knew where the hands on the clock would be. When the older brothers were in the military, Dad gave him geography lessons and I particularly remember him pointing out Australia on the globe. Once when Orvin was about two years old, my friend Jean and I were out with him alone and we had to cross an irrigation ditch that had a little water in it. We tried to get him across, passing him, but one of us missed the 'catch' and he fell in! None the worse!"

Lila relished her life in the country.

"Besides the farmland, we had an orchard," she remembered. "During the peak season, we picked crab apples, strawberries, choke cherries, and raspberries. There were three long rows of raspberries and every other day we picked them... up to 100 quarts at a time. Now I can't imagine what we did with all that. Mom canned a lot, and we gave a lot away. Mosquitoes loved the area, so we wore long sleeves. One bush by the road held berries. They were red and very bitter, but my Aunt Alma loved a bowl of them with milk and sugar when she came to visit. We had lots of hens and gathered eggs by the dozen. These were put in special boxes and divided into special sections for each egg. At the Valley Cash Store these crates of eggs were exchanged for groceries. I remember us shopping for everything we needed in the food line. While in high school, my girlfriends and I would sometimes walk to that store at noon and I'd buy a package of cookies or something to munch on and charge it. I don't ever remember Dad complaining about it, or even mentioning it. Mother canned dozens of quarts of fruit from our orchard and vegetables from the garden, and meat. Her canned beans were out of this world delicious, I thought. So cellar shelves were full of good food for the cold winter months. Canning was an art because if the jars were not sealed properly while the contents were hot, they spoiled. Spoilage was rare, though."

In spite of the rough-and-tumble life of the country, and her having only brothers, Lila was still a typical girl.

"I was definitely very feminine," she said. "I loved to clean and even cooked at an early age. The Dionne Quintuplets were about my age and were all the rage. I remember having them in paper dolls and changes of clothing in paper outfits. One thing that stands out in my mind was a playhouse I had. There was a new building in our yard that had an empty room and I turned it into my own little home. I fixed it all up, but there was a clumsy motor in there. I couldn't move it and I didn't want my cozy playhouse destroyed by its presence, so I put a white cloth over it. This brought chuckles from the adults, but that was fine by me."

Another aspect of childhood for Lila was having various fears and worries.

"We never talked about things like that," she commented, "so I kept them all to myself. As a first grader I walked to school with my two older brothers Ernie and Ray. It was a long walk across fields and I was so afraid as we came across bulls grazing along with herds of cattle. I had never heard of anyone being attacked by them, but I guess I thought I could be the first one! Once there were groups of crows cawing here and there. The boys told me they could attack people, so I was full of fear at seeing them, even though my brothers could protect me. And my parents had a friend who occasionally came with his wife to visit us. He scared me so much because he said he wanted to take me home with them. Now I know it was said in friendly fun, but in my little mind it was a scary thought! I've often thought how important it is to have children confide in us about their fears and we can reassure them and further explain things that are troubling them. Another time when I was about fourteen, I had my brother Lloyd's car and was taking some of my friends out for a ride. These were country roads and there wasn't much traffic. Coming around a bend turning a corner, I didn't quite make it, and the front right wheel veered off the road. There we sat, probably wondering how we could get back on the road, when suddenly I saw a man working in a field right near us. I thought, he could help us, but my hopes were dashed when I saw that it was a friend of Lloyd's! He did help us get back on the road, but I knew it was just a matter of time until he told Lloyd and then I'd be in trouble! Sure enough, a few days later I walked into the kitchen where he and Mom were talking and he said, 'The thy-rod on my car is bent.' I thought 'Here we go!' but didn't say a word. Then he added, 'Lila, do you know anything about that?' So I had to 'fess up and that was the end of it. My worrying was for naught."

Salvation wasn't far away from the Finsaas household, and next visited Lila's eldest brother Clarence.

"I remember standing on the old-fashioned car running board when we lived at Schafer hearing Clarence tell his best friend, Jack, that he had become a Christian," Lila recalled. "Clarence and Jack went to school together and also played banjos together, but at this point their lives took opposite turns. Clarence was teaching in a country school, but now he decided to quit that and go to Minnesota to Bible school. He told me later that he didn't dare tell Dad that he was going to Bible school. He would come home for vacations in the summer and was a great encouragement to Mom."

When Lila was eleven, she went to Watford to attend evangelistic meetings that were held at the high school gymnasium. It was about this time that she met Jean Bond who became her lifelong friend. Two singers from Clarence's Bible school led the music, and the Holy Spirit began working in Lila's heart during these meetings. After the meeting she found one of the singers, Bernice Nelson, and told her that she wanted to be saved. Lila was crying as she asked Jesus to come into her heart that night.

"Clarence took me to the station to take the train back to Fairview and gave me a little Bible," she recalled. "He also told me to be sure to tell Dad what had happened. I never did. But one day I had fallen asleep reading my Bible, and when I woke up, my Dad was sitting beside me looking through the Bible. I often wondered what would have happened if I had given him a clear testimony of what Jesus had done for me, but I was afraid to. It was a full six years before he made that decision."

Others noticed Lila's change of heart before she said a word about it.

"Mother later told me that she noticed a change in me when I came home after being saved, that I was singing around the house," she recalled, "and she said she hoped it would last. Outwardly I got lost in the shuffles of life around me, but inwardly I knew I was saved though I wasn't ready to give myself completely to the Lord. Somehow I thought I'd never have fun anymore, that life would be boring. What a mistaken notion that was. I went to confirmation classes every Saturday morning with a lot of other kids, and this was very good for me. We had to memorize a lot of Scripture. This lasted for two years, and then we were confirmed. Confirmation included questions about the Catechism and the Bible before the church audience, and then a ceremony and communion. It meant a lot to me, and I took it all seriously. We went to Williston, and Mom and Dad bought me a new dress for the confirmation ceremony."

Lila's spiritual growth continued when she went to live with the family of a friend.

"Jean wanted me to come and live with them and go to high school in Watford with her for my junior year," Lila recalled. "She was a senior. Later it seemed so strange to me that I had been away from my parents for that whole year, but I also came to the realization that this was God's way of protecting me. At home I was not living for the Lord. Living with the Bonds helped me whether I wanted to be helped or not. They were solid Christians and went to a Bible Presbyterian Church. I always went with them to Sunday school, church, and young peoples' meetings. One thing Jean and I were good at was laughing. We could laugh easily and hard at a lot of things. I don't think that one Sunday school teacher thought we would amount to much the way we could cut up. Still, Jean's parents kept a tight reign on us, and we had to live up to high standards. We went to Youth for Christ meetings on Saturday nights. I played the guitar, and we sang duets."

Newly spiritually grounded, Lila returned home for her final year of high school:

"For my senior year I went back to Fairview High school and my seatmate was a Nazarene girl, a good Christian who also became valedictorian of our class. So again, even though I wasn't so happy about it, I was stuck! These were some more guidelines from the Lord to keep me on track!"

Another spiritual transformation in the Finsaas family would once again prove to be a turning point in Lila's spiritual development.

"I'll never forget the morning Ray came home while Joe went on to his military station," she remembered. "My bedroom was just off the kitchen, and I heard Ray tell Mom he had gotten saved. I'm sorry to admit that I thought, 'He'll never be any fun anymore!' He was always joking and the life of any event. Mom told him to tell Dad. He said he had on the way home in the car, and Dad had said, 'I'm going with you.' So that was one of the first steps of showing spiritual interest on Dad's part."

That spring Lila decided to go to the Prairie Bible Institute spring conference with Joe, Ray, and her Mother's sister, Alma. The trip took them across most of Montana before crossing the Canadian border.

"On that trip we all almost went to heaven," Lila remembered. "Joe was driving, Ray was beside him, and Alma and I were in back. I distinctly remember leaning forward to see how fast he was going, and it was 62 miles an hour. Suddenly he was having trouble, the steering wheel was spinning in circles, and we sailed off the road going between fenceposts and out into a field. Joe, being the mechanic, wired up the rod, and we drove to the next town and got it fixed. Farther on we saw places where, had we gone off, we would not have lived to tell it. We have always marveled at that incident, because within ten years my brother Joe was in India, Ray in Africa, Alma in Taiwan and I in Japan – all as missionaries!"

Lila was in the eighth grade when the news came that there had been a surprise attack at Pearl Harbor. The United States was now drawn into World War II, and many Americans grew to hate the Japanese for what they had done. Becoming a missionary to Japan was the furthest thought from Lila's mind.

"Everyone was very patriotic," Lila recalled. "One by one my brothers went into the military. Norman and Marvin into the Army, Lloyd in the Navy and Clarence also enlisted into the Army chaplaincy, with part of his training at Harvard."

Marvin was the first brother to be drafted.

"He had attended Billings Business College so it was only natural that he became company clerk in his unit," said Lila. "Once he confided to Dad that with that job he couldn't advance beyond the rank of corporal.

Dad encouraged him to stay where he was because it was safer than being in direct combat. However, we learned later that he was once miraculously spared when his unit was marching across a bridge in Germany where he served with General Patton's famed Third Infantry Division. Marvin, obviously exhausted, fell asleep walking, and the soldier behind him kept him from falling over the bridge they were crossing!"

Another brother, Joe, had started at the State School of Science at Wahpeton, North Dakota, and at one time ran his own car maintenance business in western Montana. Later he too decided to attend Prairie, focusing primarily on ministry preparation. When he came home for a visit, he was promptly drafted... to train dogs in the military.

"Once he sent a big dog home to the folks," remembered Lila, "and Dad went in to the train station to pick him up and bring him home. His official name was Fritz and he came complete with official papers and tags on his neck."

Still another brother Ernest was called up next, but didn't pass the medical exam. Her Mom said had he been drafted, she would have complained to the draft board. She felt that five boys from one family were enough. Still, it was somewhat of a disappointment to Ernest.

"During those years the guys would come home on furlough, and we always took them to church with us," recalled Lila. "The church had a flag with stars, one for each man from the church in the service. Rev. Peterson always publicly acknowledged the serviceman in the audience, and we were very proud. They always looked so sharp in their various uniforms. But when they left after a short leave, we never knew if we'd see them again. They always got a short leave before being sent overseas, though this was never public knowledge. We just knew it. I remember I was glad when they left in the evenings because after I slept, I felt better. If they left in the mornings, I felt sad all day! I felt sorry for Mom and Dad. They were terribly, visibly sad, but so brave."

Lloyd, her brother who had enlisted in the Navy, left one day when Lila was in junior high.

"It was a sad day for me," remembered Lila. "Lloyd was a great tease and a lot of fun. Once he chased me all around the yard to get a peek at two cards I had gotten from a forbidden boyfriend who had also just gone into the service. Hawaii was Lloyd's eventual destination."

Yet another brother Norman was sent to the Philippines, and for a whole month they received no communication from him. While he was there he was hit by shrapnel, hospitalized, and later sent home. He was eventually awarded the Purple Heart.

"Mom was home alone the day word of his accident came," Lila recalled. "The postman came to our home and handed Mom a telegram from the State Department. Then he expressed the condolences of the community. After he left, Mom opened it: 'We regret to inform you that your son, PFC Norman Finsaas, has been slightly wounded in action.' In her haste, she read seriously instead of slightly. All day long she lived with the thought that he was probably near death. When Dad came home that night, he asked if there was any mail. She told him there was a telegram on the table. He read it and quipped, 'Well, it could have been worse.' She said, 'What do you mean?' He answered that it said 'slightly' wounded."

All of her brothers would eventually come home safely.

Lila's eldest brother and spiritual mentor was headed for a life in the pastorate and continued to provide inspiration to his baby sister.

"When Clarence pastored a church in Superior, Wisconsin, he fell in love with his pianist, Jeanette Nelson," Lila recalled. "So on furlough they were married in Wisconsin and came home to us. I was so happy to get my first sister! Then Clarence was sent to Japan, and Jeanette went to Bible school in Minneapolis. Between my junior and senior high school years, she came out to visit us. Jeanette, my Aunt Alma, and I once took a trip to Seattle. It was fun to be with them, but I remember we visited Lake Sammamish Bible Camp, and I was very uncomfortable because I wasn't ready to give myself wholeheartedly to the Lord. I wrote to a nursing school in Minot asking about nursing. However, my parents said they wanted me to have one year of Bible school and then I could go into nursing."

Lila really wasn't too happy about going across the border to attend Prairie, but her parents had other ideas. They asked Clarence to come home with a special task: to persuade her to go there.

"Clarence and I sat on the back lawn. I loved him a lot, and they knew he had a way with me," she remembered. "But I was stubborn. He said later that he almost gave up. He talked about Prairie and I said, 'Why can't I go to the school you went to?' He said, 'Well, because Mom and Dad want you to go to Prairie.' I felt that I could have bluffed my way through at most other schools, but instinctively I knew I couldn't at Prairie. He asked me why I disliked it so much. I said, 'Well, those long skirts the girls have to wear.' He countered so sensibly, 'Did you ever think that if everyone has long ones and you have a short one on, you'd feel funny and out of place?' I hadn't thought of that. It made sense. So I agreed to go."

Before leaving, she saw her grandmother for the last time.

"Before I left...Grama gave me an especially tight hug. Little did I realize that had to last...she passed away a couple of months later and they said her funeral was like a coronation."

With that, Lila made the trek to the school that would change the course of her life.

"We went by train and stayed overnight in Calgary, about 90 miles from Three Hills, taking a bus the next day," she recalled. "I had a closet full of clothes at home, but could only take the tops as all of my skirts were just at the knee. Mom hurriedly made me four skirts: a black, a grey, a red-patterned plaid, and a brown one. I put one on before we left Calgary and rolled it up at the waist about four times, letting it down when we got to Three Hills. Ironically the next year the style became long skirts. Mr. Maxwell [the principal of Prairie] once joked to the student body, "The Devil tells you to put 'em down and you do. When *we* do, it's a problem!"

Arriving at Prairie, Lila quickly acclimated to the new environment.

"We had arrived a little late, so when I went to my first Homiletics class, the professor announced that there would be an exam next time on the material covered so far," she recalled. "I knew I had a good excuse, and I got the notes from a girl and copied them. It took me all study hour that evening just to copy them. When I returned her notes and was walking down the hall, it came very clearly to me: 'Take that test.' I had never experienced anything like this, and it was just like a matter-of-fact thing. So the next day I took the exam with everyone else and to my shock, I got 100%. That was an incident that stood me in good stead the rest of my years of study, and I learned that God was well able to make up to me what I needed if I obeyed Him."

It wasn't long before something extraordinary occurred at the college at the annual Fall Conference, where Dr. Armin Gesswein from Seattle was the main speaker. He spoke mostly on the topic, "Have you received the Holy Spirit since you believed?" from the book of Acts.

"During one of the afternoon meetings, a missionary from China got up to give a report of his work. He stood with bowed head for some time, then looked up and said, 'I was planning to give you a glowing report of my ministry. But in all honesty, I can't.' His voice shook with emotion. 'All I can say is that I've been a miserable failure on the mission field,' he said as tears filled his eyes. 'Pray for me.' The missionary sat down and buried his face in his hands. His shoulders shook with sobs. We were thunderstruck. A long silence followed. Gradually, we became aware that we were in the presence of a Holy God who will not tolerate sin. One handsome young man in the balcony rose and said with a broken voice, 'I've led some of you to believe that I lived a victorious life in the army, but I did not. I failed the Lord many times. I ask you to forgive me.'"

Like a field of grain bending in a gale, the whole auditorium of people bowed low before a holy God. The wind of His Spirit penetrated every recess of their hearts, convicting the students of hidden sins, some long forgotten.

"All they could do was cry, 'Oh, God, have mercy! Oh God, forgive me. Cleanse me,'" Lila remembered. "Tears flowed. Sin became 'exceedingly sinful.' One person after another arose to confess sin in trembling voice. Since we had difficulty hearing them in the large auditorium, Mr. Maxwell suggested that they come to the platform and use the microphone. Soon a long line formed across the front and down the full length of the building. The rest remained in prayer. We were all so conscious of the presence of God that we cared nothing about people's opinions. All we wanted to do was to get rid of the awful burden of sin weighing heavily upon us. The meeting went on hour after hour. We were oblivious to time. Supper time came and went. The cooks were told to hold the meal until later. Still, people stood in line – young and old, students and staff – awaiting their opportunity to confess sin before God and man. Late that night, the principal reluctantly dismissed the meeting and said we could have dinner if we wanted to. Most of us did not. We were too overcome with the presence of a Holy God and the awfulness of our sins to care about food or sleep."

The meetings continued into the next day.

"The next morning the meeting took up where it had left off the night before," she recalled. "There was not much preaching that day; just another long line of people wanting to confess their sins. More weeping. More praying. The Holy hush of God was upon the place. It was an awesome spectacle. Some confession was done privately. Students went to teachers to confess cheating or a bad attitude. Others apologized to friends for a lack of love or for criticism. Letters of apology were written. Money owed was paid back. Borrowed books were returned. No sin seemed too small. Pride was just as heinous as stealing. Gossip was as wretched as immorality. As time went on, we felt like onions being peeled. We got rid of one sin, and there was yet another. I'm not sure how long this went on, perhaps for three or four days. We asked the Holy Spirit then to fill us as clean, empty vessels. Oh, the joy that flooded in! We almost skipped around campus."

From that group of revived students, a great army later went to the mission fields of the world to share the Good News. Lila woke up in the mornings after that conference filled with an unusual peace and joy. Before, she had believed the Enemy's lies and thought that giving herself to the Lord would mean the end of her fun. But now she was embarking on a wonderful life of living close to the Lord.

"But I also had restitution to make," she recalled. "I'm so glad I was only seventeen so I hadn't had time enough to be too wicked! I do remember after that, thinking that I wasn't doing anything I was afraid my parents would find out about! But I did have to write some letters asking forgiveness including one to my parents. Mom wrote back and said how glad she was for me and that she hoped it would 'last.' I also wrote back to my high school principal asking forgiveness for cheating on exams. Had I known that he was so touched that he read the letter to the whole assembly, I might not have wanted to go back home when school was out! He got a similar letter from another student, I learned. And he wrote me back with forgiveness for anything I remembered."

Known for its strict rules at the time, Prairie was a difficult place for some young people accustomed to total freedom. But Lila's newfound transformation made it an easy place to be.

"From then on the rules didn't bother me, and we joked about the ones that did," she recalled. "The classes were hard, but I also studied hard and learned a lot, since I felt I had a lot to learn. We also had a lot of fun in the dorms and got to know kids from all over. Rules were strict. Study hours started at 7:30, and lights were out at ten. We were up at six. Once the girls across the hall were noisy after study hours started, so I wrote them a note and told them to appear at the Dean's office on Saturday morning! I signed the name of the girl in charge of our hall. My roommate and I were watching their door and listening, and she said, 'they know you wrote it.' We went back to our studies and forgot the whole thing - that is, until Saturday morning. Heading out to play basketball in the gym, I met those same two girls coming out of the Dean's office. I was shocked and blurted out, 'Where have you been?' They said, 'It's none of your business,' but then I told them that I wrote that note. So they said they'd go back and explain. A few days later I had to see the Dean for something. She was formidable – an older lady who was totally in charge and firm. She said, 'Lila, I've been waiting for you to come and see me. This could be a demerit!' The problem was in my signing someone else's name, she explained. I never did get the demerit, though, and she kept in touch with us in Japan until she passed away two years ago."

Lila's time at Prairie was a time of deep spiritual growth as well, and in time her deep awareness of sin was soon accompanied by grace.

"I did go through a period of subtle condemnation," she recalled. "Whereas in high school I didn't have a conscience that bothered me – like the time I skipped school and went with a friend and we made cream puffs and I wrote my own excuse and signed Mom's name – now I felt guilty about too many things. Did I do that right? Was I honest in what I said? My roommate seemed to sense this, and one day I came across Romans 8:1 and read it to her: 'There is therefore now no condemnation to those who are in Christ Jesus...' And Esther strongly blurted out, 'Now take it then!'"

In April, after Lila's first year at Prairie, her family came to take her home and, while there, attend the annual Spring Conference. The radio preacher from California, Charles E. Fuller, was the main speaker. The conference was made very special because by this time, her father and brother were saved. Unknown to Lila, her future husband Kenny was saved under the same man at Soldier's Field in Chicago. Lila spent three more years at Prairie and always came home for the summers.

"Somewhere during my senior year at Prairie," says Lila, "I began to have a serious struggle because I was feeling that God wanted me to be a missionary. My idea of a missionary wasn't great. I remember telling Mom once, as a teenager, that one thing I never wanted to be was a missionary. I had never met one, so I had nothing to go on, but I told her plainly that I felt they were people who 'couldn't get any other job.' She said, 'Well, I feel just the opposite. They have to be able to do so many things!' I sensed God was calling me to be a missionary, and I really rebelled about that for a while. I did not plan to be a missionary; I did not want to be a missionary."

During this time of struggle Lila remembered having heard someone say that if there's something God is asking you to do and you just can't, pray that you would "willing to be made willing."

"So, since the thought of leaving my parents and going to a strange country seemed so outlandish, I decided to do that," she recalled. "Before I was fully aware of it, my rebellion was gone, and I was very interested in becoming a missionary. During one of my years at Prairie, Clarence and Jeanette came for the Spring Conference, and he introduced two missionaries from Japan, Anne Dievendorf and her sister Mabel Frances. They were rather famous and had stayed in Japan during the wartime years, even having to be on their own as their mission board wanted them to leave. Japan seemed to be the place God wanted me, and so I went to a Japan prayer meeting at the room of a Japanese girl attending Prairie."

Continuing her studies, Lila was mentored by various professors:

"Studying occupied much of my time, but as a senior I taught a Sunday school class of fellow-schoolmates," she recalled. "We met once during each week to go over the lesson under the tutoring of a lady named Mrs. Waldock. Her husband was on the staff in the office. Choir was also something I enjoyed and the director, Mrs. Tygert was an outstanding soloist, and just before she and her husband left for Japan as missionaries, she sang a solo at a Sunday morning service, but broke down and couldn't finish."

In her senior year, Lila wrote to TEAM Mission about serving in Japan, but they told Lila that she was too young and needed more training before they would accept her. Lila decided to go to Grand Rapids, Minnesota, and help her brother Clarence and Jeanette in their church.

"This was a great experience. I taught Jr. High kids who almost overflowed our little room in the church," she remembered. "I also went with Clarence and played the piano when he ministered at a senior citizen's home. During this time I also worked for an attorney named John J. Benton. This was a new experience, but I enjoyed it and learned a lot. I put all my secretarial training to good use, as there were no computers. He dictated letters and legal forms, and I typed them out. I also went through all the files and arranged them with new labels. He was very kind to me. I had my own knotty pine office next to his. At Christmas time Mr. Benton found out that I hadn't been home for Christmas in four years, so he gave me time off. Joe was at Bethany College and he had bought a new car for Dad, so we drove it home."

Resuming her job with the attorney, Lila faced a pivotal moment.

"Back at work the time was drawing near for me to move on and go home for the summer. Mr. Benton knew I was not there permanently, and he really wanted me to stay. One day he came into my office, sat on the couch by the opposite wall, and said, 'What don't you like about this place?' I asked him if he really wanted me to tell him. He said he did, and I said that I didn't like the profanity that went on. With the lawyers and clients there was plenty of that. He quipped, 'Well, there hasn't been much since you came!' Then he added, 'You'll never make a missionary!' I asked him why and he said, 'because you're too happy. They always look like they've lost their best friend!'"

Lila's chosen mission agency, TEAM, had a long and colorful history. In 1876 Fredrik Franson, a son of Swedish immigrants to Nebraska, went to Chicago to meet the famous evangelist D.L. Moody. He became a part of the church founded by Moody and was trained by the evangelist as a counselor. In 1879, Franson went to the Utah territory to minister to some 30,000 Swedish immigrants who had gone there for inexpensive land. Two years later Franson left on an extensive ministry to Europe where he heard the well-known British missionary statesman, Hudson Taylor, challenge people to go to China with the Gospel. From that encounter, Franson got a vision to form missionary-sending agencies in various European countries. Before he left the continent, six such organizations had come into being. After arriving back in America, Franson continued to preach. His desire to motivate others for cross-cultural missions led him to form a training class in Brooklyn, New York. His first class on October 14th, 1890, is recognized as the "birthday" of TEAM (The Evangelical Alliance Mission), although the early name for the agency was "The Scandinavian Alliance Mission."

This name reflected Franson's vision to bring churches together into an alliance, enabling even small congregations to have a part in sending out missionaries. Classes were also initiated in Chicago, Minneapolis and Omaha. Soon a formal board of directors came into being, and on January 17th, 1891, the first band of 35 missionaries boarded a train for the West Coast and eventually China. Photographs of these early missionaries depict a dedicated group of people who chose to live and dress as the Chinese did. Other groups soon joined the first recruits, and Franson fervently challenged still more to go. En route to China, the early missionaries passed through Japan, and that soon became a new field for the mission.

In a similar manner, by 1892, a small group also went to Swaziland in southern Africa. In 1908, following one of his lengthy trips to the fields, Franson took several days off to rest at the home of some friends in Idaho Springs, Colorado. One morning his host tried to wake him for breakfast, but he had died during the night. Franson left behind no family or estate. His legacy was a group of dedicated people whose desire was to take the Gospel to all people. Franson's two passions, evangelism and church planting, continue to be the focus of TEAM's worldwide ministry.

After spending a summer at home, in 1952 TEAM invited Lila to work in their Chicago office where she met many godly people, men and women, old and young on a daily basis, from all over the world.

"Ray was also a missionary candidate, and he also came to Chicago, and we had separate apartments, but shared a kitchen," she recalled of her brother. "He worked downtown for some months and then headed back home to get ready for his upcoming wedding to Myrtle. My jobs were varied as they put us candidates wherever there was a need. For a while I worked at the switchboard on Saturdays and had Mondays off. Learning this job gave me a nervous stomach for the first time in my life! Calls came in from all over, and I had to take the messages and/or switch them to the right people. And when I got used to it, the busier the better. The time came for Ray to go home, and after he left I found an envelope on the table that had his writing on it. I remember turning it over as I got lonesome for him just looking at his handwriting! In April, I took time off to go home to be in their wedding. They were going to have as their wedding motto, 'United to Serve in Japan' but decided instead on just 'United to Serve,' and that proved to be wise because they ended up in Africa where they spent many fruitful and faithful years."

Lila's job with TEAM was challenging and also contributed to her spiritual growth: "The office staff held devotions each morning in a downstairs room. One day an old Africa missionary, Dr. T.J. Bach, got up and left the room. When he came back the director questioned him. He replied, 'I just went to give Brother Swanson a hug.' Such love permeated the headquarters. For a time I worked in the filing department, which proved to be training that I've used all my life in Japan. We had to be able to find letters and records as far as seven years back, and if it was that far back, we had to go to a basement where old records were kept. Most of the mail from all departments ended up on my desk, and that was most interesting."

During this time, Candidate School was held at Trinity Seminary, a two-week course for people interested in becoming missionaries. Lila attended, along with 25 others. Several people ended up in Japan; others went to different fields.

"Back at the office, I was getting ready to set out for Japan," Lila recalled. "I had been there a year and a half, so I wrote on my quarterly form that I should soon be on my way. Shortly after that, the boss called me in and said that since I was still young, I could stay on at the office for a while yet. Then he chuckled and said that he read what I wrote, and it was fine that I move on. I went back home, and then the formidable task of deputation to raise support was before me. We had to raise promises of $125 a month, which was sent into headquarters. Clarence said I was pale when I went to my first deputation meeting. Here and there I spoke, telling people all about a land and people that I knew next to nothing about. But it was just after the war and I guess folks were glad someone was going with the Gospel to that country. Some pledged $5, some $10. My Aunt Alice wrote to the family, 'Lila stands ready to go, but she needs support.'"

Little by little promises came in, and now Lila was ready to head for The Land of the Rising Sun. The Mission made a reservation for her to leave on a ship from Seattle.

"I was with Ray and Myrtle in Lewistown on deputation, and we had some good laughs as we tried on some of the clothes. Long underwear was required! Once we bought some clothes at a secondhand store, and trying it, on discovered one of us had the dress on backwards. We laughed and said if it looked so good backwards, just think what it will look like when we put it on right."

Lila Finsaas was on her way to the unknown – and for an adventure that would last a lifetime.

# Chapter 5

# *A Big Surprise in the Land of the Rising Sun*

Much later, as an adult, the realization of how difficult it had been for Lila's parents to let their only daughter travel 7,000 miles away would hit Lila.

"Dad bought barrels and a pressure cooker for me as we had to take so much along," she said. "Something he got for me had to be put together, and I said I couldn't do it. He said, kind of exasperated, 'Aren't there any men around there?' Finally the time came, and Mom and Dad took me to Glendive, Montana, to catch the train to Seattle. A lot of my family came to say good-bye, and I walked down the line saying good-bye to each one. The last one was Dad. He was openly crying. I had never seen Dad cry before. I was crying, too, and I got on the train and sat down and was on my way. Sometime later a lady sitting next to me asked me where I was going and I said, 'Japan.' She said, 'I thought so.' Meaning that it must be more than a mere trip to Seattle! Upon arrival there, I was met by my Aunt Alma and Uncle Ted who took me to their home at a place called King's Garden. I also attended Alma's graduation from Seattle Pacific University. Future boat-mates Anna Nelson and Bessie Degerman also arrived, and we shopped and packed together until it was time to get on the boat."

Sailing for Tokyo, Japan, Lila and her friends had a blast.

"The boat trip was exciting, and we heard that the crew wondered what we had done wrong to be sent to Japan. It was a cargo vessel and didn't have many passengers. We were treated royally."

After the long 14-day sea journey, Lila, Anna, and Bessie arrived at the port of Yokohama. They were welcomed and taken to TEAM Center where a missionary couple named Mr. and Mrs. Laug were in charge.

"Someone in our group said, 'Hey, look, there's a sink,'" Lila remembered. "I guess to see running hot and cold water and everything so modern was a surprise. After all, Tokyo had been severely bombed, so we really didn't know what to expect. I went out in the countryside and visited my old Prairie roommate Esther Zerbe and her husband and children for a few days. They had finished language study and were established in their work. Then we three boarded a train and headed for the mountains of Nagano Prefecture to a little village called Karuizawa. That was the place TEAM sent new missionaries for language study, so it was all set up for us. Here were spent many special days, and lifelong friendships were established. Besides Anna and Bessie, Lorraine Reece and Pat Junker joined our ranks. Japanese teachers came to our rooms and taught us individually. We studied from a course that was taught to the American GI's. Right off we learned sentences like 'Tabaji wa, doko desu ka' or 'where can you buy cigarettes?' It got you speaking the language pretty early, but not the polite kind. (Later when I had moved to Tokyo and gathered some ladies together for a meeting, I was shocked that I could hardly understand them because their language was so polite and different from what I had studied!

Lila lived in a large house with several other young American missionary ladies and they took turns caring for the house with the help of the Japanese couple.

"Mr. and Mrs. Yamamoto were our helpers in this big house, and so helpful to us since we didn't know enough of the language to even shop. Mrs. Yamamoto cooked wonderful American meals for us, and we ate together in a good-sized dining room on the first floor off the kitchen. There was a big living room that had a fireplace. We girls took turns planning the 27 meals, gradually learning about food and cooking. Mrs. Yamamoto was a happy person, and we liked her so much. Everything was new to us. One day, a local mountain, Asama erupted. We all ran out on the upstairs patio to see what was going on. Down below were some Japanese people looking up at us and talking, but we didn't know what they were saying nor what was going on. Pat Junker, always the daring one anxious to use all her newfound Japanese, said to them, 'Wakarimasen. Keredomo, tabun shirimasen.' ('We don't know what you're asking, but we probably don't know the answer anyway!)'"

The city was busy because this was the time of year missionaries came up to the mountains. Karuizawa Union Church was the gathering place for Sunday services. There were two different conferences: An interdenominational missionary conference and a Keswick-type Deeper Life Conference. This was a blessing for Lila – and she didn't miss many meetings.

"Lorraine and I have often laughed at an incident that happened one day when we were heading off on our bikes past the Karuizawa train station," she recalled. "Out of nowhere came a good-looking American serviceman, and he was visibly happy to see two American girls in this Japanese town. We finished our errand and were heading back, when here we saw him again coming toward us. He greeted us warmly, to which Lorraine answered with some glum firmness, 'We're missionaries!'"

Lila remembered Karuizawa as a delightful place. "It had luscious greenery all around when we arrived at the end of June," she said. "The train ride from Tokyo took about four hours, and we went through 103 tunnels to get there. During our time there we rode bicycles everywhere. Also, at that time none of us wore slacks, but thankfully the hemlines were way down, so our warm coats were good for even our legs! We usually studied with a teacher and by ourselves for about eight hours a day. The evenings found us very tired. But not too tired to have lots of fun and excitement and play games."

This church had a choir, and Lila loved singing in the services. She also occasionally played the piano for the meetings. It was at one such meeting that she would meet her future husband, Kenny Joseph.

"One Sunday morning as I was singing in the choir, I saw a handsome young man wearing dark glasses come in and stand in the back," Lila remembered. "I immediately recognized him as Kenny Joseph because we had been in contact with the TEAM missionaries at the office and prayed for each one by name during our morning sessions. I was intrigued, but I had decided that I would leave men behind and concentrate on being a missionary. Having just said a firm good-bye to a young man before leaving the States, I was not fair game now. Or so I thought. Still, I couldn't get this young man out of my mind. So one day I told the Lord that if he was, could possibly be, the one He had in mind for me, to have him come to an evangelistic meeting that night where I was playing the organ. What a shock to me when he walked in the back! He didn't stay long, but he had walked in!"

"I saw her first from my bedroom window in the Karuizawa hospital here I was recuperating from an appendix operation and getting treated for tuberculosis," Kenny recalled of the first time he saw Lila. "I saw a beautiful blonde walking with other girls in the sunshine. I prayed for a week and fasted and asked for God for a green light. It was green! One Sunday evening I walked from the hospital to an evening service in the Karuizawa Gospel Hall. With my two Japanese friends I walked into the hall at 7pm. I noticed the girl standing at the door, blonde, playing the accordion."

Lila kept her "sign" from God to herself and made the young man work hard to win her heart.

"I never told a soul, and actually when he did begin to pay attention to me, he thought I was very hard to get!' she recalled "There were a lot of singles around at this time, and some busybodies were trying to be matchmakers. Some of us ended up in a Jeep en route to a meeting one day, and I was having my first prayer letter done at a printer. I got out of the car to work on this, and suddenly Kenny was beside me to 'help' me. I ignored him, feeling that I didn't need his help. He went back to the car. I later discovered that he had been pushed by the other missionaries to 'help' this new missionary."

Another time, Dr. Fred Jarvis and Norman Grubb (W.E.C.) pushed Kenny out of a car to visit her at her home, but she wasn't there.

Soon, however, Kenny and Lila were dating and an item in the missionary community.

After several months of dating, in November of 1954, Kenny took Lila by car to a famous spot in Karuizawa called "the four corners," where he proposed marriage. "We drove around looking at beautful trees making an arch over the little roads srounded by moss. I stopped, got down on my knees in the car and asked Lila, 'Will you marry me?' She was a little bashful and amused, yet she said 'yes,' and then, 'Now get up!' I bought the engagement and wedding ring when in the States.

"I had bought the engagement and wedding ring in the U.S. and we drove around looking at beautiful trees making an arch over the little roads surrounded by moss. We drove to Roppongi the "6 crossings corner" and I stopped the car and got down on my knees in the car and asked Lila, "will you marry me?" She was a little bashful and amused yet she said "yes" and then "get up from there!"

"He proposed, I accepted, and he left on a short furlough for the States," Lila remembered matter-of-factly. "During that year, we girls studied hard since two of us had upcoming weddings. Actually, it was a two-year language course, but we finished it in one year. Every six lessons we had an exam, and finally after finishing this course, we had an oral exam before a committee. One on the committee was at Prairie when I was. Of course then our Girls House members scattered, but were still in Japan. Lorraine and Buz went to Niigata, Pat and Cal to Matsumoto and we came to Tokyo. The doctor had ordered Kenny not to travel in evangelism like he had been doing, but to have a quieter job, so he taught at the Japan Christian College and pioneered the Evangelism Department for five years."

The couple was married at the Karuizawa Union Church.

"It's a good-sized 100 year old wooden building – still standing and in use – and it was full," remembered Kenny. "Lila wore a beautiful white wedding dress that was made for her. Her aunt Alma was her maid of honor. I wore a black suit just bought in America for the occasion. Don Hoke presided."

The two were married and honeymooned in the resort town of Atami, where Kenny took pen to paper and wrote a note to a supporter in the U.S.

"Lila and I are sending this letter to you from our honeymoon place. The Lord has been so good to us, and we truly seek to magnify His Name. Do pray for us as we begin the noble experiment of trying to live cheaply as one, for I will soon carry Lila over the threshold of our Japanese-style home a block from the Japan Christian College. Pray, too, for His strength, wisdom, and tact as we begin teaching and preaching and spearheading the evangelistic program and outreach of the College. We're looking for this fall to be a seam-bursting enrollment of future evangelists and pastors. You'll remember it was for these students that I spent most of my furlough raising $15.00 a month support. This money doesn't go to them simply as a gift of cash, but instead they received Bibles and Christian books free. When they need more cash, they go out house to house selling these Bibles, do effective personal work and make a commission. Though my past evangelistic campaign schedule will be somewhat curtailed by these new responsibilities, I feel that I'm multiplying myself 108 times as I try to follow Paul's advice to Timothy, "The things you learned from me before many witnesses, you must commit to trustworthy men who will be competent to teach others, too. Take your share of hardships like a good soldier of Christ Jesus. No soldier ever allows himself to be involved in the business affairs of life, so that he may please the officer who enlists Him." Well, we promise to tell you more about the wedding in our next prayer letter, to send you a picture and a surprise for Christmas. Once again a big thank you for all you've done and may His grace continue for us and Your servants for Jesus' sake as we break the living bread to these for whom Christ died and rose again."

"We went to the Green Hotel in Naka-Karuizawa, north of Hoshino Onsen," Kenny recalled of their wedding night. "It was on a hill, beautiful, quiet, restful place. While we were enjoying each other, relaxing, came word that our TEAM missionary Abe Miller's wife had died of encephalitis and they wanted our permission to use the wedding flowers for the funeral service at the same church! Unbelievable. Hatched, matched, dispatched. Here today gone tomorrow. Wow. What a shock on your honeymoon.

"Tokyo, where we settled, was very cold. I always settled near the potbelly stove when we went to the college church near our home," remembered Lila. "I remembered Clarence, who had been in Japan as a chaplain with the military just after the war, said it was so cold in Japan that you even froze with 'long handled underwear.'

"We were blessed by moving into a brand new Japanese two-story home in Hamadayama, Suginami Ku, two minutes away from Japan Christian College where I was director of evangelism and professor of missions," Kenny recalled. "From the kitchen window Lila could only see the road and rice fields but from the back window she could see the college."

"I was asked to teach at the college Personal and Mass Evangelism and Foreign Missions to Japanese from all four main islands," recalled Kenny. "There were no books or material in Japanese, and a couple of times a week the Rev. Goto and I met and eventually wrote three books: Evangelism, Theory and Practice – 26 chapters; two books on Personal Evangelism, I and II, all in Japanese."

"I had never been alone in my life. In early years it was my family, later schoolmates and roommates, but suddenly I found myself alone as Kenny was off to all sorts of places for evangelistic meetings," recalled Lila.

Lila knew that there would have to be some major adjustments in her life now that she was married to Kenny Joseph, a man who, although he was living in Japan, saw Asia as his mission field.

# Chapter 6

# *Family Life and Parenting*

When Kenny and Lila said "I do" and were joined together in marriage, they really had no idea what lay ahead for them. But they would soon learn what it would mean to raise boys in Japan.

"Lila had eight brothers so she always wanted a little sister to play with so she wanted a baby girl," recalled Kenny. "I had three sisters and wanted a little brothers I voted for a boy and so you see who won," he laughed, of the four boys who would soon join the Joseph household.

A word they heard often was "Kawai-ee" which is Japanese for cute, for as their family grew, their "cute" kids became quite an attraction for their Japanese friends. One of their sons, Bobb, recalls, "In terms of minuses of being an MK in Japan, being 'gawked over' is probably the biggest. From when I was very young, women would say 'kawaii – ne!' ('isn't he cute?!') and children would say, 'ah – gaijin da!' ('look – a foreigner!'). So we stood out and were often called attention to." The children stood out in a crowd and were often treated like live dolls. Curious strangers would pinch their cheeks and fondle their hair.

## Kimbo

The first of the four boys to join the Joseph family was Kenneth whom they later called Kenbo for short, which then became Kimbo. He was born in 1957.

"Since I had three sisters, I was so happy to get our first boy," recalled Kenny with a laugh. "Mrs. Ishihara was our next door farmer neighbor, and she let us know that to have a first-born boy was considered a good omen as was finding a white snake in the back yard! She told me one day, 'Don't carry your baby Ken across any river for the first 100 days because the river demons will catch him.'"

Lila recalled another admonition, "When I brought Kimbo home from the hospital, the neighbor lady came over. At that time we always had our babies sleep on their tummies, so I had a firm mattress and bed covers for him. My neighbor lady messed up the whole bed as she was talking to me, fluffing it up so it would be soft. I was still tired, and about this time Kenny came home from school. He sized up the situation, and while he kept talking to her, he fixed the bed back the way I had it: firm.

Lila said that Kimbo was a popular boy with the JCC students and that shortly after he was born he had colic. One day Kenny came home around 1:30 p.m. and gasped, "I'm so tired. I've got to get a nap."

Lila hit the roof and said, "You've got to get a nap and I haven't had breakfast or lunch!"

Kenny replied, "Oh you poor thing, let me take Kimbo." He did, and Lila was able to go out for a walk. "When I got home they were both fast asleep!" she recalled.

Lila said that one day when Kimbo was about two, he looked out the window and said, "Takebi."

She said, "We didn't know that was the word for bonfire! Our boys didn't know Japanese was hard. They picked it up as life went along."

When he was about 2 ½, Kimbo was, in Florida and he and his dad were taking a taxi somewhere. The driver was smoking, and Kimbo blurted out, "He's got fire in his mouth!"

Not too long after that, when they lived in their home at Eifuku Cho in Tokyo, close friends Bill and Jean Brandt visited them. After the meal, Bill "lit up," and just as Lila feared, Kimbo quipped, "He sure must love the devil!" It was quiet so everyone heard it. But Jean, who later we learned, had been encouraging her husband to stop smoking, said, "Out of the mouths of babes and sucklings," as if to underscore that feeling.

Lila recalled that as boys will do, Kimbo once ran his hands under the faucet and headed to the table to eat.

"Just a minute; not so fast," Lila said.

"I took him back to the sink and washed one hand with soap and water. Then I put his hands together – one still dirty and one sparkling clean – and asked him if he couldn't wash them better himself. He quietly looked at them both and then said of the darker one, 'I like this one better...it looks more like a Japanese.'"

One evening, Lila remembers that she and Kenny were having guests for supper, but just before they came, Kimbo hobbled out from a closet with a needle poking out of his foot! He had stepped on it.

She said, "We rushed to the hospital, and I said to amiable Dr. Johnson, 'Doctor, do you have boys or girls?' He said, 'I've got one boy and two girls and he can raise more Cain than both of them together!'"

## Kimbo

*It's your birthday!*
*You recall past ones*
*with Pee Wee and Philip and Roger and Murray*
*jumping out from behind a couch*
*Parties*
*Birthday cakes...*
*Remember the cake when you hit 18?*
*A big X over a motorcycle*
*And a car beside it*
*You could drive that*
*Finally*
*But I recall way back vividly*
*First I asked God for you*
*A prayer*
*in short and*
*in my request book.*
*Then there was the crib*
*A boy? A girl?*
*Which would it be?*
*The crib was in both pink and blue*
*Ready and waiting.*
*The first time I saw you*
*In a nurses arms*
*I'll never forget that look on your little face*
*A boredom look!*
*Later when I went for a walk*
*I felt like announcing!*
*Didn't everybody know I had*
*a baby boy?*
*You were the J.C.C. sweetheart*
*At evening time when Dad*
*rounded a certain corner*
*on his way home from*
*J.C.C.*
*He'd call*
*"Kimbo, Kimbo, Kimbo"*
*You'd tumble around*
*on the floor*
*Once a typhoon came*
*You and I were*

*alone*
*J.C.C. kids came over*
*One took you on her back*
*We went to*
*safer quarters.*
*Bobby joined you*
*Quite a pair*
*Once he came into the house*
*with a neat cut-out of his shorts*
*He'd been Saul*
*You David*
*School by bus was fun*
*To Washington Heights*
*Then C.A.J.*
*Remember you played*
*a cripple boy*
*in a play*
*Your "cane" is in the attic today!*
*Always adventuresome*
*in the middle of Japanese*
*student rebellions*
*Compassionate always*
*to people--*
*making me visit that hurt girl*
*and bringing that inebriated man home*
*for the night!*
*and the little dog you found on a*
*rainy day*
*along the road*
*Remember when you*
*and Roger & Murray went*
*to the ofuro?*
*You hitchhiked*
*Later he searched out our home*
*to bring back a sock you forgot*
*and a box of mikans!*
*That ship trip was exciting*
*as a High School Junior*
*You made beds all the way*
*to America*
*and back to Japan by*
*World-Airways*
*We picked you up*
*in the middle of the night*
*at Yokota*
*Jimmy and Markie*

*were growing*
*Four boys*
*As a senior you took Markie*
*on your cycle to school.*
*He was a 1st grader*
*He felt your hand on his knee*
*as you prayed for safety*
*College was exciting*
*Student offices*
*work with Japanese*
*New friends*
*Trips back to Japan*
*Once we heard noises downstairs*
*We called the police*
*It was you...home to surprise us*
*When they came we were all laughing!*
*You graduated with a double major*
*But the best is ahead.*
*Keep faith in God and people*
*May He use you greatly.*

## Bobb

Robert, nicknamed Bobby, later known as Bobb, joined the family two years after Kimbo on February 27th, 1959, in Tokyo. He recalls some of his earliest memories of his missionary parents:

"I remember Dad reading to us when we were little and playing with us. He read from a big, cushioned Bible Story book we called the 'Softo.' He would also play 'circus' with us, with him on his back on the floor, one of us on his outstretched hands, the other on his feet up in the air. Then he would have us run up to him, still on his back, and he'd flip us over his head behind him. Even though Dad would be gone for weeks at a time on evangelistic meetings that took him across Japan and throughout Asia, when he came home he would spend time with us doing fun things together. I also remember riding on the back of his bicycle, standing behind him on the wide, sturdy rear rack with my hands on his shoulders, looking ahead of him. This memory served later to illustrate to me how I was blessed to have a father who loved the Lord whose shoulders I could look over as I followed in his footsteps.

"And of course, Mom was always there. We were blessed to have a mother who made sure we lived at home and near school, so we had a home life, rather than live in a dormitory... I have early and fond memories of Mom tucking me in and singing to and praying with me. I remember we wanted Mom to be our 'Room Mother' at school, which meant she and a few other mothers would be responsible for special activities, like bringing cupcakes or treats to school at special events and being available to help the teacher. And it was my Mother who led me to Christ when I was nearly three years old. She was reading me a Bible Story that talked about heaven and hell. I was so struck by the horror of going to hell that I said, 'Well, Den – I hafta be saved!' My mother paused the story and prayed with me, as she had done with many Japanese women before. It was then that I asked Jesus to come into my heart and take me to heaven with him when I died."

Bobb became a great playmate for Kimbo. Lila remembered a day that Kimbo and Bobby came in from play. "We noticed that Bobby's cute little blue outfit had something wrong with it," she said. "This one-piece, seersucker material shorts with little suspenders had a neat cut-out of about an inch along the hemline in front. We should have known that they were acting out a Bible story, and Bobby was Saul sleeping in a cave when David came so close that he could cut off a piece of his robe and so prove that he was not out to hurt Saul!"

During this time Bobb missed his first days of elementary school having caught a cold.

"One morning I guess he thought he was ready to go back to school, so he took his temperature and he brought the thermometer to me – still in bed – to check," said Lila. "I jumped out of bed in shock as it registered 104 degrees! He had washed it under hot water!"

Bobb spent nursery school at an American military school and kindergarten at a Japanese school.

"During my one year in a Japanese kindergarten, although I obviously stuck out like a sore thumb as the only non-Japanese in my class and the school, I enjoyed it and made friends," he remembered. "I spoke Japanese fluently, and I remember being treated like just one of the other students. Since it was a Christian-based kindergarten, we prayed and sang Christian songs, including at mealtimes. I still remember two of the songs (Chiisana ote-te o... and Hibi no kate o...), which I helped my children learn and we used them sometimes at our own dinner table!"

After that, Bobb spent all his elementary and high school years at Christian Academy in Japan (CAJ) with the exception of furlough in the USA. "I always felt like an American," he said, "though blessed with the ability to speak Japanese and engage with people in their own language."

One time when he was in the 6th grade, his teacher sent home a note saying she thought he needed his eyes checked.

"We took him to an eye clinic, and he was soon wearing glasses," said Lila. "Dark-rimmed, classy ones. What surprised us was that a new world opened up to him. Then came the time to switch to contact lenses. We all suffered with him as he tried hard contacts a few hours a day. What a change when he got soft lens contacts."

Lila remembers the time she was studying Japanese with a teacher at their home and a Japanese lady had taken Bobby, then aged three, out to play at a park during that time.

Suddenly the phone rang and she said, "Bobby has been hurt."

"We asked her to grab a cab and come on home, which she did," Lila recalled. "Where was he hurt? How? Badly? It was a traumatic time until the cab pulled up, and we got in and took him to the hospital. I was happy to see that it didn't look too serious. A swing had hit his mouth and teeth.

"At the hospital the doctor pressed two teeth back in place and put a couple of stitches in his chin. I remember he said, 'I can tell that you don't lie to your children.' 'How?' I asked. 'Because when I told him it wouldn't hurt, he believed me, and when I told him it would, he also believed me!'

"The teeth stayed in place for the normal length of time. One front tooth was just a little dark."

Lila also recalled the time when the family was in Florida on furlough and Bobb was in the 2nd grade. His teacher was impressed with his background and life, so in order to get him to talk she asked the class to tell what their father's work was.

"I guess by the time he had heard doctor, teacher, office manager and others, he didn't know how to similarly categorize his Dad, so he said his Dad did 'nothing.'"

One of the downsides of being an American in a foreign country was missing out on mainstream American culture: "We missed out on some experiences that our fellow Americans had, Bobb remembered this was somewhat mitigated, however (this would be a plus!), due to having mostly American friends at school and having many popular American TV shows in Japan (Bewitched, Lassie, Superman, etc.), though remarkably accurately dubbed into Japanese. The pluses, however, far outweighed the minuses. Since Americans were highly regarded and respected after winning WWII, most Japanese thought well of us from the start – you might say we were treated with favorable discrimination. It was assumed that we were honest, good, and kind, unless we showed otherwise. "The safety of living in Japan was a great advantage, too. We could go virtually anywhere on our own as elementary through high school students – on the train, bus, driving, etc. – without fear of danger or crime. One summer during high school a friend and I took a cross-country bike trip but ended up hitch-hiking with truckers and others who would take us. Once we had dinner with and spent the night at one trucker's home and he drove us out for a few hours the next day. There was never a fear or cause for alarm.

"A third plus was the blessing of living at home and commuting to school at the Christian Academy in Japan. Thanks to Mom's insistence, we lived a short commute from school. This allowed us to have time with the family including breakfasts and dinners at home, spend time with the family in the evening with family devotions, reading, and TV."

### Bobb
*Today is your birthday*
*Stages of you are*
*indelible*
*on my mind*
*Your beautiful curls*
*"Lila, he looks just like a girl,"*
*My friend Anna scolded*
*So off went the curls*
*Playing with Kimbo*
*Going on furlough*
*Suddenly sick one night*
*in New York*
*High temperature*
*But you'd be all right*
*"to declare the glory of God"*
*I was assured.*
*Back in Tokyo*
*Dad registered you*
*for nursery school*
*you were only 3 ½ years old*
*But you thrived*
*on bus travel and school*
*Then Japanese kindergarten*
*at Eifuku Cho*
*The only gaijin*
*What a time we had*
*Notes, directions, data*

*all in Japanese*
*Then C.A.J.*
*New friends*
*New challenges*
*You held the door once*
*while Andy stuck out his tongue*
*at the teacher*
*She was a tough one*
*But taught you beautiful*
*penmanship*
*The little violins*
*you and Kimbo played*
*hang on our wall now.*
*You were practicing*
*"Twinkle, Twinkle Little Star"*
*when a telegram came*
*Grandpa went to heaven,*
*it said*
*There were parties*
*And the play when you*
*carried a shield*
*Recitals*
*You played the piano for*
*6$^{th}$ grade graduation*
*When did pole vaulting*
*take over?*
*And walking on your hands*
*across the gym floor*
*You still hold the record for that!*
*Remember when you slipped out*
*a window at school*
*and took off for somewhere...*
*And got a detention*
*Were you class president then??*
*Was that when you*
*were called "Maito?"*
*The 1,977 5-yen pieces*
*strung on your wall*
*That day finally came*
*You took them to a bank*
*It was 1977!*
*Graduation from high school*
*You and Jim traveled across America*
*Prepared to meet robbers*
*at every turn*
*You met only cordial*

*relatives*
*and farm animals*
*College time came*
*The bass guitar stage was fun*
*Your music group*
*traveled to churches*
*Again a Montana trip*
*you, Kimbo and Jim*
*But you were itchy to get back*
*The reason?*
*You had just met a special girl...*
*you wrote your Dad*
*that you didn't know her well yet*
*but "give me time." You came back to Tokyo*
*She came to Tokyo*
*One day I was making the beds*
*You came upstairs and asked*
*"Mom, what do you think if I ask Georgia*
*to marry me?"*
*You two went out for dinner*
*at the New Otani*
*A call came," All went as scheduled."*
*Dad and I got flowers*
*and we had a party when you two got home*
*at midnight*
*You graduated together*
*And then the beautiful wedding*
*June, 1982*
*Lots of memories; lots of challenges ahead*
*Today on your birthday...*
*know that we love you and your Georgia more than words can say*
*And pray God's continual guidance, blessing on you two.*

## Jim

Lila had a difficult time with the birth of her third son James, nicknamed Jimmy, and later known as Jim.

"He was born as were all of the others at the Seventh Day Adventist Hospital in Tokyo, and had we not had an excellent doctor and been in a wonderfully well-equipped hospital, he wouldn't be here and I might not be either," Lila remembered. "Everything was normal until delivery time. During that period Dr. Nelson came and said to me, 'The baby is coming chin first and he can't be born that way. We'll have to give you a spinal.' He did, and from then on, it was easy. Jimmy arrived, and Dr. Nelson was checking him. I found out later he was checking to see if his forceps had been a problem. When he saw that was not the cause of the problem, he breathed a sigh of relief and quipped, 'Well, he'll be all right.' Then I heard the nurse ask, 'This, too?' I wondered what was behind that question. When I was back in my hospital room, the nurse brought Jimmy in, and he had a bandage on his head. Soon Dr. Nelson came in and told me that Jimmy had a dent on his forehead, but that it was 'purely facial.' It was not eight o'clock yet, but he said he had consulted his textbooks, counseled with other doctors, and talked to a surgeon at Yokosuka Naval Base. He said he had never seen this before, but the Yokosuka surgeon had, so if we agreed, he would do the surgery. So in two days, Jimmy was taken by a missionary lady to Yokosuka. The surgery was performed with only a small incision in his hair as an instrument was inserted to lift up the dent. Dr. Nelson explained it thoroughly to me, and so I was confident that the Lord would guide the surgeon."

"Jimmy was five when we moved to our present home in Oizumi, and the lot next to us was a forest which he dearly loved to meander around in," Lila recalled. "He'd catch little wild animals for his planetarium. And he'd take plants to the neighbor ojisan (Japanese for Uncle) and ask him their names. "In that little forest he loved to putter around with his cap on backwards. He kind of wanted to be a farmer in those days. But when Mrs. Kobayashi, our next door neighbor, spotted his latest trophy – a snake he bought in Ikebukuro – and asked him if his mother knew he had it, well, she found out, and he didn't have it very long after that! "But the day came when Jimmy stood looking out the dining room windows as workers began removing his favorite haunt: the forest. I can still hear his deep inner groan when the tree cutters slashed the first tree down. It was a Sunday morning. That was the beginning of the end – now houses are there!"

Bobb recalled a funny moment with his younger brother: "When we attended Sunday School at a local church, I was in a class Jim, who was about five at the time. He was shown pictures of animals and told the Japanese name of each one. When it came to usagi (rabbit), they said, 'Kore wa usagi desu' ('this is a rabbit'). But Jimmy's stubborn streak came out, and he said, 'Kore wa RABBIT desu!'

While Kenny may have been unsure of his parenting skills, having had no brothers, Jim remembered special moments with his Dad:

"We were on furlough in Florida and I was missing my friends at CAJ. I felt my life coming to an end. Dad took me aside and sang me a song:

"Count your blessings." No matter what your circumstances there is always something to be thankful for. It was a big deal to me and am grateful that God had me learn that lesson early. Dad trained us to look up to and admire people that the world looked down on and vice versa. He trained us to choose our heroes wisely. While the world admires John F. Kennedy and Martin Luther King, Dad saw sexually promiscuous leaders who squandered their talents for a whiff of perfume. While Jerry Falwell and Ronald Reagan are dismissed as intellectual lightweights Dad admired the courage of a man with unpopular ideas and the power of a man with the will to change the minds of an audience. I recently took my three children to the funeral of Richard Wurmbrand who fought communism and was tortured for Christ in Romania. He was a good friend of Dad's and as I was driving to the funeral with tears in my eyes I explained to my kids how my Dad looked at him as a hero and how important in this day leaders with feet of clay, that we as fathers point to the right men as heroes. Often the men that fathers point to, as heroes become the heroes to the children."

### Jim

*The cap. The gown. The diploma.*
*All a part of graduation.*
*The papers. The reports. The exams.*
*All behind you.*
*A lot of other things are behind you, too.*
*It's not hard for me to recall them.*
*One by one.*
*I can see you tending your little garden.*
*Searching the "forest" for plants.*
*Wondering, "Shall I be a farmer?"*
*Asking the ojisan for yet another plant's name.*
*Welcoming your little brother.*
*Then off to school with your two older brothers.*
*And four more Jim's in the same class!*
*And some more papers. And reports. And exams.*
*Basketball was fun. Getting haircuts was not.*
*Slipping out of church early on Sundays.*
*To make tea.*
*Having your own motorcycle.*
*So huge, heavy and fearsome.*
*A torn pant leg and a minor cut.*
*Outward signs of the accident.*
*God protected you.*
*Hitchhiking with Doug.*

*Two months.*
*"Where do we stay tonight?"*
*English classes. Dozens of new friends.*
*The sobetsukai. The signed flag.*
*And then a cap. A gown. And a diploma.*
*And an ocean to cross.*
*A new way of life.*
*And some more papers. And reports. And exams.*
*"Why can't I have my parents here. Like*
*other kids have?" you sometimes wondered.*
*But you kept going. Ahead.*
*And that moving ahead has brought you to today.*
*To the cap. The gown. And the diploma.*
*And the same precious Lord Jesus Who brought you*
*To today will never lead you on.*
*"I will never leave you nor forsake you."*
*The past was good. But the future is better.*
*"Thou wilt show me the path of life;*
*In Thy presence is fullness of joy."*
*Look ahead with humility. With anticipation.*
*With faith.*
*We are proud of you. Very proud of you today, son!*
*With your cap. Your gown. And your diploma!*
*– Love and prayer,*
*Mom and Dad*

## Mark

When Lila was expecting her fourth son Mark (known as Markie), the family went on furlough to Chicago. During their time in Chicago, Lila went into premature labor. Fortunately she was able to stay in a hospital for a day, and her condition was stabilized. Mark waited until it was time and was born on January 27th, 1968.

Lila recalls that when Mark was about three years old, she and her son were about to go out to do some shopping, but she couldn't find the car keys.

"We looked, but couldn't find them and so we prayed," she said. "But despite that, I still couldn't find them, so I suggested that we go on my bicycle. Mark marched kind of triumphantly beside me as we headed out the door quipping, 'God didn't answer your prayer!' Suddenly I remembered that I had left them on the front seat in the car and I jubilantly answered, 'Oh yes He did!'"

The four boys grew up in a time of social unrest in Japan which included anti-American protests on the streets of Tokyo. "I'm a radical," four-year old Mark announced with put-on toughness as he emerged with his brother's helmet on and a towel wrapped around his face. He was mimicking what we'd heard about day after day in Japan.

"Five young 'radicals' took over a company resort house in a mountain town that we know so well and held the 31-year old caretaker's wife captive for ten days," Lila recalled. "The final siege was a day long battle covered live on TV. A storekeeper told me his customers were half the usual as people were glued to their TVs. Two policemen were killed by the young men's' shots and a third man wanting to offer himself as a hostage in place of Mrs. Muta was also cut down.

Finally, after battling floor by floor, room by room, using tear gas and tons of water, policemen captured the culprits on the third floor and freed the weary but well captive. Besides this, there have been other 'radical' riots and uprisings, so Markie knew a lot about what he was copying!"

Lila spoke about the time when Mark was about five when the family returned to their missionary work in Japan after a year's home leave. "One day he and I were on our way to the dentist whose clinic was a walk from the train station," she said. "As he trudged along holding my hand, he asked, 'How far is it, Mom?' Without realizing that he was busy juggling two languages and cultures, I absentmindedly answered, 'Oh, about a quarter of a mile.' In a little while he ventured, 'How far is it now, about a dime of a mile?'"

When Mark was in nursery school, he brought two salamanders on the palm of his hand to show to the class. He enlightened Miss Louise, "This one is pooregunant, and this one is almost pooregunant!"

Later, when Mark was a teenager, he and Lila had a disagreement one evening – about what, she couldn't recall.

The next morning after he had left for school, she found this note which read, "Mom, I always tell my friends that if there is a difference of opinion, my Mom is always right. But this time you were wrong!" We never brought up the subject again," Lila recalled with a laugh.

Lila remembered a church friend who was a bit eccentric: "We had a friend who came to church and sometimes visited us. Mark called him 'Loony Tunes' because he was a bit eccentric. When New Year's time came, who should give Mark an o-toshidama (New Year's gift) but Tadaki San. Mark began to feel guilty about what he had called him and came to ask me what he should do about the gift! I told him to thankfully accept it, but more importantly, I think he learned a great lesson about branding people that didn't fit the usual stereotype."

## **Mark**

*A cap, a gown, a diploma*
*They're all yours today*
*All part of that great event*
*Graduation*
*Your coming was a big event for us*
*And for your three brothers*
*They each helped raise you with lots of love*
*Daddy ombu'd you*
*And you guided him with your little finger*
*While sitting under Mom's chin*
*In the car*
*Kimbo took you on his bike*
*And later on his motorcycle when you were a senior*
*And you were a first-grader*
*You felt his hand on your knee*
*And you knew he was praying for your safety*
*On Tokyo's busy streets*
*An indelible impression*
*"Babba" you called from your crib*
*And Bobby would come and get you*
*And when you'd yell*
*"Would somebody please..."*
*Bobby would always come uncomplaining*
*You monkey'd with things in his room*
*So he put up a sign*
*"Please don't touch"*
*But you couldn't read*
*And how you loved to copy Jimmy*
*Number 12 for one thing*
*Whatever Jimmy does bugged you*
*But you shot baskets*
*Jimmy was there taking pictures*
*The nigiyaka years flew by*
*You became an only child at home*
*But you were fine*
*Close to your brothers by letters*
*And*
*"Can I call Jim tonight?"*
*Or Kimbo or Bobby and Georgia*
*Yes, you got your first sister four years ago*
*So loving and caring too*

*You've had "lots of friends"*
*And kept busy with school*
*With Roba Tsushin and Hi-BA*
*And modeling and basketball*
*With trips to Okinawa and Hawaii*
*And with Mrs. Kiker*
*A Mike to Singapore Airlines*
*The 44 points were exciting*
*And other awards*
*You can give them all back to Jesus*
*And keep moving ahead*
*The past was good*
*But the future is better*
*I will be with you*
*While at the same time I will go before you*
*Jesus promises*
*He's a great and wonderful friend and Savior*
*Don't forget Him*
*And he's got a big job for you*
*A job only you can do*
*In a lost word*
*With only your one short life*
*We are proud of you son*
*So proud of you*
*With your cap, your gown, and your diploma*
*Our love and prayers*
*Will always be with you*
*Precious Mark*

## The Neighborhood

Shortly before Mark's birth, in December of 1967, Kenny, Lila, and the three boys moved to a new home in the western suburbs of Tokyo near the train station of Oizumigakuen. The 2,000 square foot house was unusually large for a Japanese home, having six bedrooms, and was owned by an artist. Since Japanese homes usually have little value apart from the value of the land, the owner offered to tear the house down so that Kenny and Lila could build the house of their dreams.

"We told him to leave it as it was," recalled Kenny, who later added a seventh room for Lila to use as an office.

It wasn't long before the Joseph kids had their first run-in with a new neighbor, Mr. Tachi.

"We gathered from their conversation that the boys had 'told off' our new neighbor," Lila recalled. "Apparently, Mr. Tachi had reprimanded the ones who were playing in the backyard, probably for letting the basketball hit his house or just for general noisiness. Kimbo was in his room upstairs overlooking this event, and he went to bat for his brothers by opening his window and telling the neighbor in perfect Japanese to 'get lost.'

"After talking it over, we decided that they needed to go and apologize. So the two little boys, Kimbo and Bobby, took hands and slowly headed toward Mr. Tachi's house, rang the bell and told him they were sorry. Obviously impressed, he answered in English, 'You guys are great.'"

Lila remembers other interactions with neighbors.

"When we moved to our present house I saw Kimbo watching a neighbor lady pour salt over a nearby ledge. This is a superstition to avoid accidents. But, anxious not to cause trouble with our new neighbors, I asked him, 'Kimbo, did you say anything to her?' You can guess what he asked her by his answer, 'She said she didn't even believe it!'"

## Never a Dull Moment

There was never a dull moment for Lila as she tried to raise her sons the best she knew how. She relates, "Oh how I loved my little boys! They were my life. I was hands on. And usually they were put first, but I remember one Wednesday night I was chiding, 'Hurry. Finish eating. I have my class, you know...' when one of them – I think it was Jim – threw out, 'I hate Wednesday nights!'

"From then on I tried to be more careful about the whole Wednesday night situation so they would feel relaxed and more important than the class! I always felt that if you lose your kids, your ministry doesn't have much value. But, being an imperfect mother, I failed in lots of ways. We had to learn on our own most of the time...Lorraine, Pat and I!, us old roommates who got married out here and were raising our families. There were no pertinent seminars to go to and not a whole lot of books on our needed subjects. But I've always said that I couldn't have loved them more... I did have my own joke, though. I said that if Kenny had married my aunt Alma, there wouldn't have been anyone home to raise the kids because both were world travelers."

"At night a ritual was 'love talks' on their beds before they fell asleep. Sometimes I think I might have over-used this opportunity to 'teach' them something, like when I was leaving Kimbo's room one night and he quipped, 'I only asked a question. I didn't ask for a sermon!'"

*Once my Bobb and I were riding on a bus in Tokyo's loop,*
*It was crowded to the doors and if we tried we couldn't stoop;*
*All he saw was belts and buckles, but I saw above the throng,*
*And though the trip was irksome, still I knew it wasn't long.*

*But my little Bobb was frightened – to be wedged in oh, so tight,*
*The rest were so much taller, he was just a little mite.*
*All around him it was darkness and he couldn't see ahead,*
*He could just stand still and trust me; clinging, waiting to be led.*

*But he learned a little secret-he'd look up into my face,*
*And my smile of reassurance would his worried look erase.*
*Bit by bit the bus then emptied, Bobby saw a shaft of light –*
*Joyfully he inched out to it, now he knew that all was right!*

*As for me, I saw a lesson: God is in supreme command,*
*And though I cannot see or fathom, I will trust and hold His hand;*
*Though the steps to take are shadowed, and I search in vain for light,*
*I'll keep looking in His face–and be assured 'til faith is sight.*

Lila recalled a time when Bobb was between age two and three, and the boys had a goldfish that died. They buried him in the backyard, and there was a little mound to commemorate the event. One day Lila saw from her kitchen window that Bobb was kneeling in front of the buried goldfish. She half jokingly called out, "Are you praying *to* it or *for* it?"

He promptly answered, "To it."

She thought to herself, "Time for a furlough!"

The Joseph family spent many summers in Takayama, a city in the mountainous region of Gifu Prefecture. It has retained a traditional touch like few other Japanese cities, especially in its beautifully preserved old town.

"One summer there we had a near tragedy," Lila remembered. "The three older boys had gone down to the ocean to swim, and I cleaned up our cabin and then went to join them. But before I got there, Jimmy had gone out in water deeper than he could handle. His friends thought that he was only fooling when he called for help. But Dave Springer, the lifeguard, saw him struggling and sped out and rescued him from drowning. We'll always be thankful for Dave's quick help!"

One day, Lila was cleaning Kimbo's room and found a strange note.

"I never delved into their private belongings," she said, "but this was out in plain sight. So I called him at school since it bothered me. 'Oh

Mom, I found that note at Yokota (Air base)!' he answered. That made sense!"

Lila remembered that Bobb was always neat, "but he had a little brother who rummaged around in his room while he was at school," said Lila. "Short of locking his door, he decided on another solution. The main problem was a low shelf that held his boxing gloves and other important items. So above the shelf he put a sign, 'Please do not touch.'

"The only problem was that the only one who touched it, Mark, couldn't read!"

## Girl Trouble

"Mark's first grade teacher said he had teen-age problems in first grade!, Lila recalled. A girl came in crying and when she asked her why, she had said that Mark told her she couldn't talk to any other boys!"

She remembers other times trying to prevent the boys from growing up too fast:

"'Have lots of friends' was a common theme at our house! What it really meant was, 'Don't get tied down to only one girl so you miss having lots of friends during these formative school years!' I remember reminding one of them that 'you still have at least eight years of school left...' The next day I was walking down the hall near the CAJ office. Around the corner and coming toward me were two of them! But as if a gun had gone off between them, they went their separate ways! We never mentioned it!"

Furlough presented some interesting situations as well.

"When we were in California on home leave," she said, "one day one of my sons and I were out shopping [and he] took me to the jewelry section and asked me if I'd buy two necklaces for him. One said, 'You're the only one' and the other said, 'I love you.' I told him I'd buy him one of them, but not two. He dropped the subject and so did I as we moved on. A short while later I was cleaning his room when I happened upon two small packets ready for mailing. With them was a note to his older brother, 'Please mail these two for me, but don't tell Mom.' So I guess they were mailed and the brother never told Mom!"

As the youngest sibling, Mark was the last to graduate from high school.

"When we were on home leave living in La Mirada," wrote Lila, "Mark was at a stage where he didn't want to be different from the other kids. So he told no one that he was born and raised in Japan. His teacher happened to have had a couple of home stay students from Japan the summer before so she was most interested in that country. One faculty member was a young Japanese man so she went to him and began asking him about Japan. He said to her, 'You have a student in your class who is from Japan. Why don't you ask him?' She did – so the secret was out – and she became a special friend to our family.

## School Days

The boys grew older and went off to college one by one. For Lila, letting go was always hard:

"Jim's arm was draped around my shoulder as he groaned, 'Mom, let's pray. Bobb and Kimbo are all leaving and it just hurts inside.' He put his hand on his chest. Since they would all be crossing the ocean from our home in Japan, this was no small parting. All had been here for parts of the summer and now it was time to head back to school in California. Bobb would be the first to leave. We prayed that the Lord would help us as they all left and we stayed behind. I tried to be the 'brave one' in the days that followed. But I was aware that Jim (16) and Mark (11) were having a battle. I thought about Bobb leaving. My mind wandered and I could see him as a child in 6th grade. He wore dark-rimmed glasses, and they seemed to fit his studious, organized personality. I'd think about it and tears would surface. What was it? Was it crossing the ocean that made it so hurtful? Whatever it was, it was mastering us."

"I comforted the boys, 'The best is yet to come. God has many happy things ahead for us yet.' But they were hollow words. I was already lonesome for Kimbo and Bobb and they hadn't left home yet. I thought of my Mom and how brave she managed to be as we left, one by one. She never cried in public, but I knew it hurt her so much. But I bet I'll cry, I thought. And then it happened. I remembered that the blessed Holy Spirit is called our 'Comforter.' So I prayed differently than when I prayed with Jim. I reminded the Holy Spirit that He was our Comforter and that we desperately needed His comfort. Then I forgot about it. Looking back later I just marveled at how the Holy Spirit did meet us and took away completely, that grief, the dreaded upcoming loneliness, heaviness – whatever it was that had enveloped us for a while and threatened to swallow us up. The last night all, four boys slept side by side on mattresses on the living room floor with the air conditioning on. Their upstairs rooms were hot and humid. We decided to get a picture of this. Bobb set the camera and then crawled back onto his mattress. But it wasn't a sad evening. We laughed.

For lunch the next day they wanted Russian Piroshke, a family favorite for special occasions."

Although parting was hard, Lila felt God softened the blow.

"And then it came time to gather up the suitcases and head for the airport. I can't explain it, but we were far from a grief-stricken bunch!" she recalled. "We were free to say good-bye happily. The Holy Spirit was comforting us. Surely we needed to be a praise-filled group. Bobb was off to college for his third year. He had spent part of the summer counseling at a Bible camp, and had made so many new friends, and during the summer renewed old ones. Two came in cars to take us all along to the airport, and when Kimbo left later, we handled that with grace, too! We should be sad? No, we would be happy! We would rejoice, and we did! As each one left, we who were behind were free to help them instead of thinking of just ourselves! The Holy Spirit really did comfort us!"

## Parenting

Lila Joseph had come to Japan to devote herself to the work of Christ in a manner not unlike the vows taken by nuns who commit themselves to Christ and His work. But life had handed her a different set of cards, and she had made the adjustment from missionary to missionary-Mom – fiercely protective of her family and committed to their physical and spiritual well-being. One day Bobb said to her, "If there were three of you, one could rest!" Lila's philosophy of parenting was a combination of the values of honesty and hard work learned on the prairies of North Dakota and Montana and the worldview she would later acquire at Prairie. She drew particular inspiration from L.E. Maxwell, the president of the College.

A central tenet of Lila's parenting philosophy was that she had no right telling others about God if her own children weren't following Him. It was part threat, part parenting technique when she would announce to each of her four sons that if they were to get into serious trouble on the mission field, the whole family would return to the U.S.

Another fundamental in her parenting technique was that children, especially missionary children, must not be sent to boarding schools of any kind, and she steadfastly refused to even consider such an arrangement.

While her parents had both been good parents, her Mother's faith had often been a lonely one that was developed outside of her husband's knowledge or approval until later in life. It thus fell to the man Lila lovingly called "Mr. Maxwell" to provide her spiritual grounding.

"The hardest thing to maintain is balance," she would often quote her mentor, among many phrases that would pepper her parenting. With Kenny often gone, preaching internationally, it was often left to Lila to parent her growing family. She devoted herself to her cause with equal amounts of love and devotion.

As a mother, Lila is often praised for her parenting skills, but when asked about that, she responded with characteristic modesty: "I did the best I could considering that we were so much on our own. I had lots of friends both at home and in Japan, but we were all far removed from each other. And there weren't a lot of books to help us in our particular situations. And we had no e-mail! And telephone calls were expensive... so rare. I tried to let my boys have as much free reign as they could handle, and I feel they handled it well... riding motorcycles, modeling shoots (one said that he would tell the Japanese group right at the onset of a trip that he didn't drink or smoke, so that was good and settled). Another son said once, "Well, you didn't always have the right answers, but we saw your life."

"I learned from them too," Lila recalled. "One day I was steaming about something and walked into a son's room. He could have said, 'Mom, cool down!' Instead he came with, 'Do you remember those Praise books we used to read?' That was a gentle rebuke I needed to hear. I think we all grew and learned a lot together. And I always said I couldn't have loved them more than I did and do. It encourages me even today when we are an ocean apart, to remember hearing our Georgia, newly married to Bobb, say, "I've never seen boys love their mother like these guys do!"

A gathering of pre-war missionaries to Japan pose in front of the Karuizawa Union Church in 1933.

This photograph of General Douglas MacArthur towering over Japan's Emperor Hirohito was released shortly after the Emperor renounced his divinity in a radio broadcast to his people

Kenny's mother Martha was a prayer warrior whose prayer closet was said to have had two holes in the carpet from where her knees had been

Lila poses with her mother Julia who came to faith after a near-death illness

Kenny with a friend at Bob Jones College in Cleveland, TN

Lila receives her commission as a missionary to Japan from TEAM Mission's Dr. Mortenson

Kenny, honored at a Youth For Christ banquet in 1950

After finishing college, Lila worked as a legal secretary and then at TEAM Mission headquarters before leaving for Japan to begin mission work.

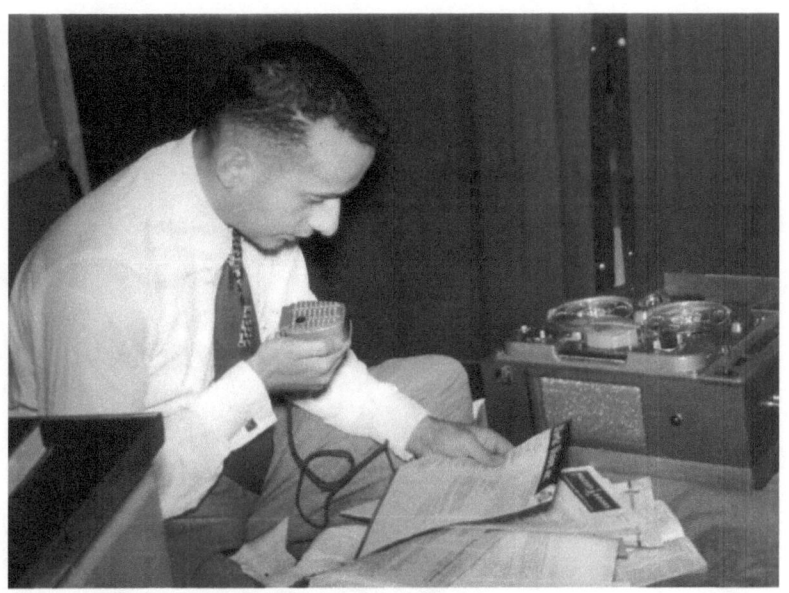

Kenny prepares for an evangelistic meeting

Shortly after arriving in Japan, Kenny began traveling around the island nation, preaching

Kenny & Lila's First Christmas Card, Announcing Their Wedding In 1955

Newlyweds Kenny & Lila pose in Japanese dress

Kenny launched his publication, REAP Magazine with the help of hardworking Japanese co-workers

Kenny enjoying a traditional Japanese meal on a train trip across Japan

New Parents: Kenny & Lila show off their first son (Ken) Kimbo

Jim, Bobb & Kimbo enjoy time with their Dad in a backyard pool

The Joseph Family 1968: Kenny, Lila, Kimbo, Bobb, Jim, Mark

The Joseph boys: Kenneth Philip, Robert Samuel, James Orvin, Mark Scott

Lila playing the piano at Grace church which began meeting in the Joseph's home in 1976

Preacher Boys:
Bobby and Kimbo

Kenny and Mark pose in front of their snowman in the backyard

Lila passing out tracts on a busy Japanese street

Kenny passing out tracts in front of a Shinto Shrine

Kenny standing in front of the Reap Center which would later be embroiled in controversy

Kenny wearing the traditional face mask which Japanese wear to prevent colds from spreading, rides the train to work

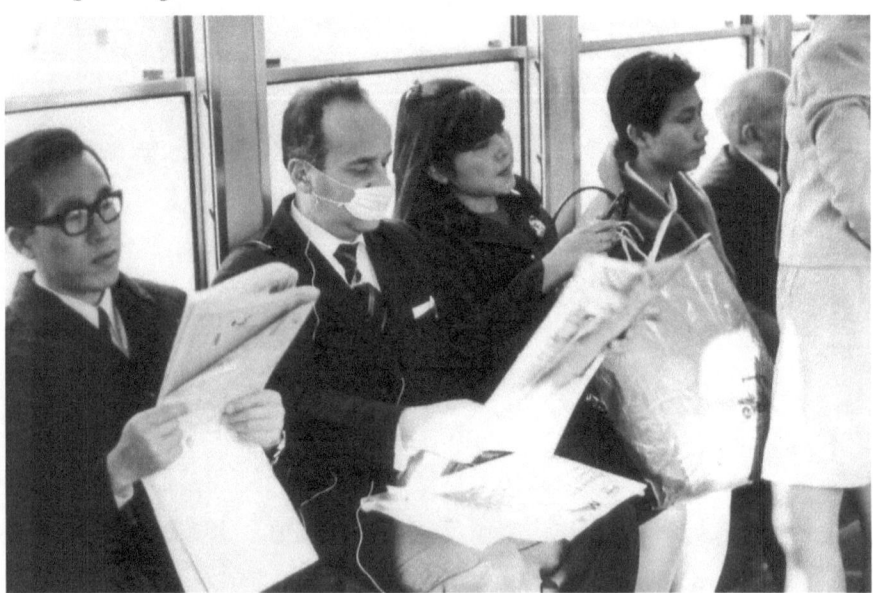

Lila speaks at a Ladies Luncheon

Lila and her sons: Mark, Kimbo, Jim, Bobb

Kenny Preaching At a Japanese Church

Kenny began performing wedding ceremonies when he discovered that they provided him an opportunity to minister to non-Christian Japanese who could hear the Gospel in a non-threatening environment

Lila prepares lunch for church members with a co-worker, Mrs. Takehara

The Joseph family in 1995: Jim, Mark, Bobb, Kimbo, Cindi, Kenny, Kitto, Lila, Jacko, Kerrigan, Georgia, Reid

Kenny at work in his office/study

Lila relaxes with a cup of coffee in her living room at Christmastime

The Joseph clan in 1998 at Mark & Kara's wedding: l-r, Georgia holding Lydia, Bobb with sons Reid, Kerrigan, Kimbo, Kara, Mark, Lila, Kenny, Cindi, Jim, son Christopher, daughters Jacqueline and Julia, Marks dog Gumby.

Kenny & Lila pose in front of the Karuizawa Union Church, a half a century after they were married there

# Chapter 7

# *Philosophy of Missions*

While his family was growing up, Kenny continued his widespread mission work. He was always helping others and supporting the work of Christ. Soon, Kenny became the editor of Japan Harvest, a magazine published by the missionary community to provide helpful information to the entire community.

"I worked under Don Hoke, a classmate of Billy Graham is and Bob Walker is at Wheaton and then Christian Life editor," said Kenny. "Don had 153 students at JCC (now Tokyo Christian College), and he asked if I could edit the quarterly missionary magazine."

However, Kenny still made time for his family: reading stories to the boys, taking them on bike rides, and working in his office part-time.

Kenny became so busy in his work in Japan that he was wearing four "hats" at the same time. They included being a TEAM missionary, a professor, editor of the missionary magazine Japan Harvest, and founder of JEOM (The Joint Educational Opportunities for Minorities Program.)

"I remember having four different letterheads, so dividing my time between those four made a busy schedule," Kenny recalled. "I had to write and ask top missionary leaders for special articles. The magazine was aimed at the 2,000 missionaries in Japan. I had it sent to the entire group, and then I got subscriptions. It was in English with ads. When the Billy Graham crusade was held in 1967, we had a special 50-page issue. It was a lot harder and took more time than I thought it would."

After his tenure as editor of Japan Harvest was up, Kenny moved to start a magazine of his own in 1961 which he initially called *Ripe*, and later renamed *REAP*.

"There were no computers, faxes, or copying machines or printers in those days. Just the one lone secretary typing using carbon paper – six to get out seven letters," he recalled. "You can't imagine the hardship of typing articles with carbon paper and with the printer, making corrections but making more errors, so we had to proofread four or five times and then we would then go out and get ads."

*REAP Magazine* would continue until 1973 before Kenny took a hiatus from publishing, which he resumed in 1982 when a friend began publishing a similar magazine, *Japan Journal*:

"I finally gave up after twelve years and into this vacuum came my fellow-missionary John Terry, who launched *Japan Journal*, saying that *Japan Harvest* was 'Pablum' and we 'need a hard-hitting magazine,' he recalled. "He made me Associate Editor. This lasted for five years, financed by his teaching English at four universities."

Kenny's work in publishing extended to his own books, which included the much in demand *Missionary Language Handbook*, which gave missionaries basic coping skills to deal with the difficult Japanese language.

"Fellow missionaries Russell Stellwagon, Dave Martin, and I, along with Rev. Goto, put out the *Missionary Language Handbook* (bilingual) so that any successful missionary would carry three black books to the meeting: his Bible, song book, and the Language Handbook. The second Handbook was trilingual with Japanese writing on the bottom. It sold out so quickly that they couldn't figure out why. Then we discovered that Japanese students at International Christian University were studying it backwards, reading the Japanese and then going to the English to prepare to go to America."

As Kenny began to develop REAP, it became clear to both him and TEAM Mission, where he head spent 16 years, that it was time to move. In 1967, he was allowed to leave the mission and start his own mission, which stood for Reinforcing Evangelists and Aiding Pastors.

"I kept getting invitations to preach in Asian countries, and that was not the regular missionary set-up," recalled Kenny. "You were supposed to stay and hoe your own row in Japan. For these overseas crusades we had already organized REAP On furlough I raised support for 50 of the JCC students, asking for $15 a month for each, so REAP was an extension of that. And instead of raising money for Japanese churches, I was raising money for Indonesian pastors. When REAP Mission was asked to sponsor a Korean missionary, I said, 'Great, this doesn't cost us a dime of support. He's coming supported and will work part time to help support himself until his church gets on its feet. Then the church will support him fully. This is a win-win situation.' In this way, we've helped support many foreign pastors. And they're on their own and doing great. I always encourage them to reach out to the Japanese, as well as their own people. And they do. Once they get their ministry going, they have simultaneous translators, and those who can't understand Korean use earphones. They like to set up their churches near train stations or shopping centers, which unfortunately is the most expensive part of town. It is an amazing financial challenge, but they face and meet it. We spent two years on furlough, and REAP ended up as a Mission within a Mission. TEAM's Dr. Mortenson decided it was best to organize REAP outside of TEAM and wrote a beautiful letter telling all of our supporters of the change and re-routing our monthly support to REAP Mission."

Starting a new mission meant that more support staff would be needed, and soon a missionary secretary, Bonnie Rose, arrived.

"Her dedicated work allowed me to minister to the people in the church and left her to pound the typewriter eight hours a day along with Lila and others while I pounded the pulpit," Kenny laughed. "She kept the books in order... and once a year at our annual conference we took out three or four days to look over the past in order to review and preview, at a Japanese inn, where we ate on the floor."

A prayer letter from Kenny during this time painted the picture, and gave supporters an overview of the work he wrote.

"Another goodbye, let's me get out into the back country of Japan where the people and the farmers sometimes have never even seen or heard a missionary, where they're steeped in idolatry, we're happy to work with existing church going out on invitation, hold a crusade, show Gospel films in Japan.

"We're also a member of the Asia Evangelist's Crusade Team holding crusades in Asia during the World Olympics. And now come with us to a church in Korea, can you believe it, a thousand people. The Korean choir is bigger than most of the Japanese churches. A thousand people come at three different times on a Sunday morning to hear us preach and go home, and another crowd comes.

"Our greatest crusades were twenty-five years in ministry and twenty years on the mission field; we're in South India where we were invited by the oldest church in the world. And we preached to more people in one night – twelve thousand – than most missionaries preach to all year, or sometimes in five years, in Japan. No television, very few movies, and so our Gospel films of life, death, and resurrection of Christ were well received. Crowds wherever we go.

"Our co-evangelist not only showed the films but preached his heart out. And at the invitation time, our Gospel team never had enough hands, enough pencils, enough decision cards, enough lights where the people could sign their names. Crowded in front are the boys and the girls and in the back the adults. A choir will sing for half an hour before the meeting starts, to keep the people happy, not only in India, but in Sri Lanka, Vietnam, Singapore, Indonesia, and wherever we were invited to bring the Gospel.

"Pray for almost a billion souls in Asia, where I serve as the International Secretary of the Asian Conferences of Laymen, Christian ministers, Christian anticommunism crusades. We are kept busy working along side as a scaffold to bring the Gospel to these even infested places, where they believe that if they can just torture themselves enough in Malaysia, somehow God will be happy.

"We have converted your money and your stamps into Gospel tracts – 55 million of them. We put them up in tract racks like this, we pass them out hand by hand, our boys Kimbo and Bobb and Jimbo are passing them out one by one. But at this rate we'll never be done. And so we go into nationwide magazine. Two million readers will read this Gospel tract in this magazine as a full-page ad, and already 23,000 have requested further information to get a free Bible correspondence course. Praise the Lord – twenty years of evangelizing in Japan."

"Almost 46,000 decisions have been made through our preaching and our literature. And now REAP sends out some more Japanese missionaries. A hundred and one have gone, like a dear brother and his wife who are in Ecuador, our former secretary and student.

"REAP the harvest while the time is here. REAP the harvest, sew in tears, and REAP with joy. And we ask you will you keep on holding the ropes as we go down into the pit and REAP some more souls for the Lord Jesus before He returns."

In an article called "The Story of Japanese Foreign Missionaries – Born in Revival," Kenny noted the importance of sending Japanese out as missionaries: "Can you believe that Japan's post-war foreign missions began at that soul-winning Tent Meeting Training School at Shizuoka. I saw the potential of young Japanese as missionaries, not only in their homeland, but also overseas.

"One of the classes was 'Foreign Missions.' Of the thirty-three students, five were called to the mission field in a student-initiated prayer meeting: Toshiko to Taiwan, Jokura to India, Yokouchi to Singapore, Horikiri to Bolivia, and Ozaki to Ecuador.

"That was how JEOM (Japan Evangelical Overseas Mission) started. We met weekly with Christian businessman Tsuyoshi Tadenuma and prayerfully planned Japan's foreign missions. After sending out Rev. Reiji Oyama to the Philippines on a "repentance mission," it took off.

"One by one they came, 'Send me to Brazil, Peru, Indonesia.' We told these volunteers to ask their denominations to start a Mission and send them out. The Free Church did, followed by the C&MA, AG, TEAM, etc. JEOM became J.O.M.A. (Japanese Overseas Missions Association).

Kenny went on to say, "Rising nationalism, anti-Westernism, anti-colonialism, encircling Islam, exploding population, and retreating liberalism have changed the climate of 'who sends and who receives.' 'The missionary obligation is no longer the monopoly of the West or the special preserve of the potential of traditional missionary organizations."

Kenny asked three basic questions which formed his philosophy of missions:

> 1. Can the "Lord of the Harvest" call, commission and thrust out as foreign missionaries, nationals from the "younger" churches of present mission fields in obedience to the first Commission?"
> 2. Can these foreign missionaries scripturally be sent out to other fields while their own country is not yet completely evangelized?
> 3. What type of training, internship and screening is right for the health of the indigenous church?

He also worked off of five basic definitions, which supported his missionary work:

> 1. Mission: "The sending forth of men with authority or commission from God or the church to spread the Gospel (John 20:21) and administer the sacraments. "Christian mission" is the proclamation of the Gospel to the unconverted everywhere according to Christ's commands.
> 2. Missionary: "One who is sent on a mission; an agent or emissary, sent to propagate religion especially," or "do educational or charitable work in some place where his church has no self-supporting local organization; hence, one who spreads any new system or doctrine." "A person sent out by his church to preach, teach and proselytize in a foreign country, especially in one considered to be heathen."

3. Older churches: or "sending or giving Churches," means those older, established churches or mission agencies which send out foreign missionaries, money, Bibles, build native churches, schools, hospitals, presses, etc.

4. Younger churches: or "receiving Churches," those newly-formed indigenous churches on mission fields which should mature toward the four-fold ideal of self-supporting, instructing, governing, and expanding their own faith in home missions and foreign missions.

5. Evangelize: "To evangelize is to present the Lord Jesus Christ in the power of the Holy Spirit so that men shall come to put their trust in God through Him, to accept Him as their Savior and serve Him as their King in the fellowship of His Church."

Kenny's five basic assumptions were:

1. The Great Commission, written in all languages and addressed to all Christians, must be obeyed by all true believers in all lands, with no exemptions.

2. Since there are only 42,250 active Protestant foreign missionaries trying to evangelize 6 billion people, an obvious need exists for more experienced, evangelical, effective missionaries today.

3. The Lord of the Harvest also calls nationals from younger churches in today's mission fields to go "into all he world and preach the Gospel to every creature. (Mk. 16:15) They must obediently go, even though their own home missions program is not completed, as did the Apostle Paul, the Eastern Church, Count Zinzendorf and William Carey, and today's Western missionaries.

4. Evangelical leaders in the sending societies, missionaries on the fields, and national leaders are privileged to work with the Lord of the Harvest as He purposes to call out a people for His Name from every tribe, tongue, kindred, and nation before His return.

   a. Home missions: Evangelizing the people of similar tongue, not only in their own country, but also overseas.

   b. Foreign missions: The "younger churches" must also reach out in foreign missions to people and countries different from their own in language, food, culture, customs and race.

Looking back today, Kenny was also clear about what he had regretted when it came to his mission work: "My greatest heartache fifty years later is that Koreans, Japanese, and Filipinos have missed the main point or the 5th point of Missions going to different countries, speaking different languages, eating different food, ministering to different cultures and people, he recalled. To a large extent, the 300 Japanese missionaries into 24 countries and over 10,000 Korean missionaries into 40 countries are not doing numbers 1 and 2. Japanese first reach out to the Japanese natives, Koreans first reach out to the Korean restaurant and get the owners to pay the fabulous rent near a train station. But the restaurant owner can't keep it up too long, and the missionaries go back home. The Filipinos do the same. I know. I've sponsored them and preach in their churches."

# Chapter 8

## *Women's Ministry*

Kenny wasn't the only one doing mission work in Japan, and Lila's work wasn't limited to raising their children, for in the early 1970's, she began teaching English to Japanese students and also instructed them in Bible studies.

"I was invited to teach English at Nihon University by Dr. Sasaki, but there was a very strong anti-war student movement at the school," Kenny recalled. "We thought it might cause trouble for an American man, but not for an American lady, so Lila taught there for several years."

She also continued to open up her home to women in her community.

"It's not like we came yesterday and we don't understand," Lila said. "They know that we understand, and so they feel like they can come with their problems, because we feel like we do understand a lot of the background of where they're coming from."

One of Lila's students, Chitose Ozawa, agreed: "If I have a problem, Mrs. Joseph gives her heart to me and my burden or problems are healed. Mrs. Joseph told me a lot of things about Christianity, and I have grown up very much."

"Lila-Sensei [Japanese title used to refer to or address teachers] seems like kookie [Japanese term for 'air']," said Kimiko Sawada, another lady whom Lila has counseled. "Becuase like air, she is always here. I can always depend on her to listen and talk with me if I have a problem. There's always an assurance in my heart that she's here, and I can call or come by. Mrs. Joseph is really well known around this area of Tokyo; in fact, most people recognize her name. If you want to know how I really feel about her, she's like my own mother, my number one best friend or a very close relative."

"God's Word is being shared everyday here in the Josephs' home. In Japan, that is very unusual," added Harumi Kato. "Many people have deep hurts and needs that they can't share with their friends or families; these things are usually never talked about. We are so blessed materially and we have everything that we need, but in our hearts, there is something missing. In Japan, people lack feeling or compassion. There's really a lack of love, but something is happening in this house that changes people's hearts. People come to share their feelings with Mrs. Joseph, and she really understands, and she shares like nobody else can. By talking with her, people can find through the Word of God what's missing in their hearts. Maybe they haven't been loved in Japan."

"These people open up, and often we can help them see what the problem is," added Lila. "Their hearts are really hurting because of unfaithful husbands. There is a common thread running through the lives of people, and once you touch that thread, you can get to their inner source and find out what's causing the problem."

One of the biggest shocks that Lila experienced on the mission field was when she was confronted by demons among the women she ministered to. While she was at Prairie Bible Institute, she learned the the motto, "Prepared for War," but thought it was a bit silly. But when she began to experience spiritual warfare in Japan, she no longer felt that way.

"One day I dropped in at a lady's house where my boys were teaching her sons English," she recalled. "These were wealthy people, really nice people, and this beautiful, classy lady said to me, 'Do you believe in demons?' Before I could answer she went on to say, 'The demons come to me every night, and they are trying to kill me.' I had never heard anything like that. Our experience with that family opened the eyes of our whole family. We saw someone who we got to know personally, someone who was obviously, and by her own admission, demon-possessed.

"One day, she said she was given three spirits, and she gave me the names of them, and I wrote them down. She started to come to church and she would have seizures. On one occasion, she and her son were in church, and this beautiful, well-dressed lady would go into these trances. One day she was in one of these states, and Kimbo was upstairs, and church was going on next door, so I went up to him and said, 'Kimbo, are you strong enough to help me?' I didn't mean physically, but I meant spiritually. And downstairs she was in the middle of a spasm, where the demons would just take control of her and talk through her. I had never experienced anything like that. So Kimbo came and we were talking and we were telling the demons to leave her. And then Kimbo said, 'Why won't you leave her?' And through her voice they said, 'Because we still have work to do.' Kimbo asked, 'What kind of work?' and they said, 'It's too bad. We won't tell you.'

"We had this older Christian lady who was a chiropractor who lived not so far from us, so I thought of calling her, but she didn't speak Japanese, so I said to Kimbo, 'Ask them if they understand English.' And she relayed what the demons said: 'If it's about God, we don't understand it even if it's in Japanese!' Finally Kenny came and we all prayed with her. She had accepted the Lord at one point, and she'd bring her Bible to church and had it really marked up, but then one day she told me, 'I am a Christian, but this house is Buddhist, and so we're going to have to follow that.' So she stopped coming to church.

"One day, she came to a ladies' meeting at my house, and there was another lady there was was off her rocker, who had looked like she picked her clothes out of the waste basket in the morning, whereas this lady was perfectly dressed with expensive clothes. And the one that was poorly dressed was pregnant. And lo and behold, afterwards, the well-dressed lady called me from her home and said, 'I'm in terrible condition.' And so I said, 'Ok, I'll be right over.' And so I jumped in the car, and I went over to her house. She was simulating pregnancy, saying her back was hurting like she was pregnant. Somehow or other, the demons from that lady had come on to her! It was all new to us. We had never heard of anything like this before. She was rubbing her back like she was pregnant, but she wasn't. And so I thought, 'I can't deal with her,' so I decided to take the two women with me and go to see my missionary chiropractor friend and have her pray for this situation.

"So we headed out in my car, and lo and behold, I had two flat tires right in front of her garage. I had only had one flat tire in my life, and that was in Montana. Imagine, two flat tires. It was like the Enemy didn't want us to go! So we began walking back to the well-dressed woman's car, so she could drive us. And all this time we're walking; she's rubbing her back like she's eight months pregnant. We got in her car and went to this lady's house, and we prayed for her and then this guy came over from the church and he prayed for her, too. And at one point, she said, 'They left!' and she swept her hands in the air."

"Kimbo...actually saw her in one of these spasms, and I could tell that once she was into one, even when she was in the car. She would clench her firsts as if the demons wanted to hit me, but she somehow kept tight control.' She knew the names of the 'gods' she had been given, and they spoke through her."

Lila recalls that as she was leaving the chiropractor's home. As she was going out of the door, she heard a voice in her inner state clearly say, "You were responsible for that meeting. Here take this!" At the moment she slammed the door on her thumb and lost her thumbnail.

Lila said, "So we knew for a while there, that we had stepping into really bad territory where we weren't wanted... Eventually, she had a measure of deliverance, but she didn't want to pay the price, so I haven't seen her now for years. They were wealthy people, and they had everything going for them, but they ended up with a divorce and he died and they lost their home. But that really opened our eyes to understand things we never understood before.

"Once, I met two women who told me that when they get together, the demons would talk to each other and it would make them want to vomit, Lila recalled os another similar incident. So finally, they put a stop to that, and when they put a stop to it, it would make her sister run to the bathroom and vomit to get rid of them. She kept telling them to leave her. She would say it like she was gagging."

"All of this made us aware that there is spiritual warfare whether we see it or not," Lila added. She was being "Prepared for War!"

For Lila, however, effective preparation also included understanding and learning to appreciate local customs in order to get along in Japan.

"Your rabbit got out and the next door neighbor brought him back, better give her a gift," was the greeting Lila's friend gave her when she got home one day.

"Invited guests, or those who just 'appear,' always come armed with a beautiful bouquet of flowers, fresh fruit or something equally special. You will remember to do the same when you are the guest. Businessmen, though coming to see the man of the house, usually bring a box of cookies, crackers or a tin of fragrant tea for the family. Not only must a bridal couple think of their own needs, but provide an attractive shopping bag of gifts for each family that attends the wedding. This bag usually contains one nice item, like a lacquered plate appropriately inscribed for the occasion, and a small lunch. A similar surprise awaits each one attending a friend's recital. Some freshly made cupcakes or a plate of cookies taken to a neighbor is always reciprocated with something special. The plate is never returned empty. Even the bereaved are not exempt. It's customary to take a gift of money to the closest relatives just before a funeral. But then in the weeks that follow, they will return to each giver an item worth about one-third of that amount. Middle-of-the-year gifts are the order of the day for those you're indebted to, like a teacher, and there's another gift at the end of the year! In any culture it's rude not to accept a gift.

Sometimes, Lila's work in Japan extended to people from other countries who had settled there.

"I once got a call from a woman and found out she was living downtown. The reason she called was because of domestic violence, and she didn't know what to do since she had only recently come to Tokyo from America. I asked her if she could get on a train and come out here. She said she couldn't because she had a black eye and a broken toe! I asked, 'Do you have some sun glasses?' to which she said she did. And the toe, well, she could walk on it. So she said she would come to our stop, Oizumigakuen. I picked her up at the station and we took her out for supper. She was a delightful lady, and we had a great time getting acquainted with her.

"When we got home, I showed her to her downstairs bedroom and eventually we three hit our respective sacks. She asked if she could call her husband to assure him that she was ok. For some reason I got up in the night and came downstairs, something I rarely do. I saw that her light was on... it was midnight. I went in and she was lying in bed with the phone in her hand. I asked her who she was talking to and she said it was her husband. Obviously this call had gone on for hours. I slipped the phone out of her hand and told him she was in bed and going to sleep, so good night! She said his talking switched from nice, cajoling, to mean, but wouldn't let her go. Since she was an important writer for a major American newspaper, this was even more difficult to understand. "It turned out that she had married this man too quickly. He was married and had two children when they met on a trip to New York. He came back to Japan and divorced his wife, but, understandably, he missed his kids.

"She stayed with us for a few days until her brother and sister arrived from New York. I was impressed with their family unity – when one was hurting, they dropped everything to come and help. One day I went with her to her apartment under police protection. During the time she was with us she kept getting calls from someone in Bangkok, so I asked her who that was. 'Oh, that's my brother,' she said. 'He and his wife are missionaries over there.' Well, we have lots of cult missionaries and I wasn't sure what group they might be with, so I asked her. When she told me that they were with King's Garden Ministries I was jubilant and whooped, 'Oh, they've been praying for one more in the family to be saved, and it looks like it's going to be you!' I knew that was a good organization because my aunt and uncle taught and worked there.

"When the family got here, they took over and all went back to the States. She and her husband were soon divorced, and she eventually remarried. We often saw her articles in the paper, and though we've lost contact, we trust she has come to know the Savior of her brother and his wife."

These types of relationships gave given Lila many "children" in Japan.

One of Lila's close friends told her on the phone, "I'm you're daughter, you know." Junko said, calling from a relative's house where she was visiting.

"I must admit to being proud and happy to have a 'daughter' like Junko," Lila said. "Yesterday she came over and after supper sat down to the piano to accompany our class in singing hymns. She practically made that piano talk/sing as she moved up and down the keyboard with runs and beautiful chords. I was practically in tears. Some of my feelings were no doubt related to the long road Junko has traveled. A road that we've had a part in. Once I had just gotten back from America and was looking at the clock to see how soon I could 'justify' going to bed... with jet lag. Suddenly the phone rang and it was Junko. She said she was locked out of her home. She lived two hours away, but I told my husband that I would have to get on the trains and go to help her. I went and when I got there, we went into the home together and I was quizzed by her husband on why I was there, but the incident blew over. Junko had a lot of episodes like that. This lady who used to work in the Prime Minister's office, was a piano teacher, a beautiful and dedicated Christian, a skillful maker of hand ornaments... had a marriage that was in shambles and she eventually felt helpless to change anything. When it seemed as though her very life was at stake, when some of the terrible headlines we read about today might be in the offing, Junko moved into our spare downstairs room and for over a year commuted to a job two hours away. After a year when the marriage was officially over, Junko moved back to her home country roots and began life with her parents. The years have flown by and her three children are grown up – one is a registered nurse, one a public school teacher, and her son is a company worker. As adults they are understanding, and love their Mom! They also take good care of their Dad. It was a trip to see her first grandchild that brought her back to her family. And to us. This morning in the car she 'lectured' on the necessity to learn to be joyful and happy and praise the Lord in spite of problems in life. She's learned it well. Junko is a vibrant person...and I'm thankful she's our 'daughter,' even though we joked that this new baby, her grandchild, is our great-grandchild! Are we that old?"

As Lila counseled with Japanese woman, suicide was always a prevalent theme in many of their lives. "'What a beautiful girl!' was my first reaction at seeing Yoneko many years ago, Lila remembered. She was then about ninteen years old and a student at the Christian college where my husband taught. But soon I realized there was something drastically wrong with her. The girl with the beautiful face had no legs! And she was missing an arm!' Yoneko's life was fairly normal until she was sixteen. At that time her mother died. This is a shock to any home, but to an Asian home even more so. Fathers often leave as early as seven in the morning and get home as late as midnight, so to the mother falls the family, home, community affairs, and money handling. So now Yoneko came home from school to a dark, empty house. There was no warm welcome. No attractive table spread with the evening meal. Nothing but emptiness in the house and in her lonesome, aching heart. How she longed for her Mother's understanding presence. Eventually her father, older brother, and sister came home, and together they got the evening meal ready and the necessary work done. But as the days went by, they sensed Yoneko's extreme depression. They tried to be cheerful. It didn't help. She began to hang out at a roller skating rink with other restless young people. This soon led her to smoking, drinking, and skipping school. All of this was unknown to her family.

As the ache persisted, one thought began to dominate her mind: Suicide. Guided by dark, unseen forces, Yoneko finally made her way to a train station in the heart of Tokyo. Here she brought her horrible plan to fulfillment: she threw her body onto the train tracks just as a train was approaching.

It was no accident that when the train threw open the emergency doors, a man standing nearby held a rope. With a deft, well-timed leap, he rescued her and tied the rope above severed limbs to keep some measure of blood in this mutilated body until more help was available.

Soon Yoneko found herself in a hospital bed. This was no comfort to her who had gone to such an extreme measure to try to die. It wasn't until she went to take some pills that she found out that three of the fingers on her right hand were gone. And then she realized that her left arm was gone from the elbow and soon after when they rolled up the bed, she fell forward. Then she also knew she had lost both legs at the knees. Now her despair knew no bounds, and she began to plot another dark scheme.

Though death had cheated her once, Yoneko decided to try again. Another way. She began to stash away the little white sleeping pills, putting them here and there so no one would find them.

However, during these dark days, a missionary, together with a young Japanese man, began to visit her. They sang and read from the Bible. Yoneko wasn't even courteous. She didn't even want to be alive, to say nothing of entertaining visitors! But each week they came. She liked the singing, but nothing about Christianity. They brought her a cassette tape, and it was while listening to that that she made her decision to ask Jesus to come into her heart.

On a concluding visit, the two asked her to pray. She did, and they left. The next morning Yoneko awoke a new person. Gone was the pent-up bitterness, frustration, and hopelessness. In turn, her life was filled with peace and love. It was a miracle! She decided it must be because she had reached out to a living God, and He had touched her. Yoneko decided she had to tell somebody, so she told her roommate. Jesus Christ had heard her prayer, come into her life, and made her a new person. Her happy disposition was almost contagious, and she learned how to do most everything. She went to the United States and was fitted with artificial legs.

For Lila Joseph, these were just some of the stories that kept her going and continually made her realize that her work and the work of other missionaries, though discouraging, was important nonetheless.

Chapter 9

# *The Great Commission is in Japanese, Too!*

The aroma of food, ready for the evening meal, mingled with the scent of magnolia blossoms. And there was something else, something disquieting to the peace of this North Manchuria evening in 1949. A Japanese Christian businessman, Tsuyoshi Tadenuma, could hear the muffled sound of Communist gunfire in the distant hills. It was the beginning of the end for Japanese businessmen like him, for China's freedom, and for 8,000 western missionaries.

"Lord, I will have to leave this country I love, but I want to be remembered as a sweet scent for You," he prayed. "Please let me come back to this country where I was born, not as a businessman, but as a messenger of your Good News. Surely, Lord, You have a better master plan than to depend only on western missionaries... Lord, how can we evangelize our billion fellow-Asians?"

A peaceful assurance came, "Offer Asian missionaries to the Lord of the Harvest for overseas service. Send missionaries from Japan just as they send out missionaries from England, America, Germany, Canada, Australia, and Sweden."

"He realized that The Great Commission is written in Japanese, too," said Kenny.

"After he was forcibly repatriated almost penniless to southern Japan, Tadenuma attended a Lutheran church and dabbled in various businesses." "When the bottom fell out, leaving him with $1.16 in his pocket to feed his wife and three children, he chanced on a tract on the reward of tithing, by a U.S. chaplain. 'Lord,' he prayed, 'Either Malachi 3:8-10 is true or I can't be an honest Christian layman. I'll start right now.'"

Kenny said that Tadenuma tithed his first 12¢ to his little church, and the Lord proved Himself to the businessman. Moving to Tokyo, he helped his old pastor, Rev. Shinpei Nobata, build a church next to his house. He fanned his vision of Japanese missionaries into a flame by reading biographies of Hudson Taylor, Mary Slessor, C.T. Studd, and Timothy Dzao. He prayed, "Do it again, Lord, do it again!"

Meanwhile, in a Christian school in Japan, four students made it clear to their leaders that God was calling them specifically to missions in India, Nepal, Brazil, and Korea.

"I shared this with a group of Christians gathered for a Thanksgiving service," said Kenny. "They responded with a love offering for the four students of 3,650 yen, equivalent to ten dollars US at the time."

But, he said, some demurred. One missionary told the volunteers to forget their visionary idea of going overseas when there were 94 million heathen right here. "Wait about 100 years till we evangelize Japan and then you can think about missions overseas."

One of the volunteers asked, "Pardon me, sir, but where are you from?"

"New York. Why?"

"Pardon me again, but is everybody in New York Christian?"

"Oh no, of course not."

"I see. Then, kind teacher, you should follow your own advice and fly back to New York... evangelize there first, then come back to Japan."

"They couldn't be talked out of it," Kenny recalled. "But it was a year later before I met a lay man who had a vision of sending out Japanese as foreign missionaries. We put feet to our vision, He gave 1,000 yen, and I produced that 3,650 yen from the Thanksgiving offering. A Japanese orphanage sent an offering collected from the orphans. An inaugural constitutional meeting was called, and the Mission was formally organized on August 31$^{st}$, 1956 by some Japanese who had been missionaries, to China, Manchuria, Formosa, the South Seas, Indonesia, and Hong Kong. The name Kaigai Senkyo Kai (Japanese Evangelical Overseas Mission-JEOM) was chosen. (The first overseas missionaries from Japan had gone to Okinawa in 1891, but immediately after the War, 'overseas missions' were rarely spoken of.) Meanwhile, in Indonesia, the Lord of the Harvest spoke to Chinese evangelist, Dr. Timothy Dzao. When Dzao and Tadenuma met, Dzao said solemnly, "I'm convinced one of the reasons our sovereign God closed the door of China to missionaries is because most missionaries didn't teach us to be foreign missionaries. We were taught to be preachers, teachers, doctors, nurses, farmers, evangelists, but seldom foreign missionaries. Please, Brother Tadenuma, do not make that same mistake in Japan."

When JEOM unfurled their banner, they felt winds of criticism from some. Kenny Joseph said that one man wrote a long letter denouncing the plan as contrary to the New Testament, and ended with his exegesis of Acts 1:8. Comparing Christ's commission to a four stage missile, the first stage being Jerusalem, second, Judea, and so on. "Not until the first three stages are evangelized can you possibly think of the fourth."

Mr. Tadenuma's answer was humble but clear. "I don't know my Bible as well as you do. But I can find no 'missiles' there. I do find two-wheeled chariots. One wheel is home missions and the other is foreign missions. Your trouble is you only have one wheel on your chariot – that's why you've been going around in circles and talk of your seven believers in ten years. Hitch on the other wheel, challenge your believers for foreign missions and drive down the perfect will of God."

When finances loomed as an insurmountable problem, Kenny had answers.

"You've given nothing. That's why Japan is like the Dead Sea – no outlet, no revival, no blessing. You can't out-give God. If you have no money, you can still give something... give used postage stamps." Thus began an amazing SOS (Save Old Stamps) campaign for missions. Japanese began to give their stamps, their prayers, then their yen, and finally their sons and daughters to the Lord of the Harvest. JEOM sent Rev. Saburo Omori as their first post-war missionary to Taiwan. His survey trip there showed an open door for a humble missionary to do "works meet for repentance." On his return to Japan, Omori shared, "As I apologized for the atrocities of my fellow-soldiers, deep hatred finally turned to love. In Taiwan, I had preached in Chinese fluently, but there was absolutely no response. Finally the Chinese pastor spoke, 'I know why no one comes forward, because I hate you, Mr. Omori, and all the Japanese. You killed my wife and only son. But God just told me to forgive you.' He broke into tears as he hugged me. As a result of his willingness to forgive an enemy, twenty-three of his congregation came forward."

A similar miracle of the Holy Spirit happened in the Philippines to JEOM missionary, Reiji Oyama. He had contracted TB upon graduation from seminary. While lying in bed reading the biography of Mary Slessor, he prayed, "Lord, of the Harvest, I solemnly vow that if You heal me, I'll be Your missionary to Southeast Asia."

"The Lord healed him and led him to start a church in Tokyo that grew to 110 members," continued Kenny. "Remembering his vow, he answered JEOM's call to mission work in the Philippines. Though no formal diplomatic relations existed to give a Japanese more than a two-week tourist visa, he miraculously received a four-month visa. He trusted for a one-way boat ticket. Up to six hundred believers met to pray for him at 6:30 in the mornings. Small gifts began to come, 88¢ from a leper colony, $1.27 from a TB hospital prayer group and he was able to get a round-trip airplane ticket."

At his commissioning service at the Ochanomizu Student Center, Oyama said:

"For 100 years now we've been receiving books, Bibles, missionaries and money with our right hand but we've given nothing with our left. In the next century, let us give... and be blessed."

Filipino evangelist, Greg Tingson, introduced Oyama to his people where he was given the opportunity to speak to thousands. As in Taiwan, smoldering hatred turned to love, and souls were saved as another Japanese humbled himself and washed his fellow-Asians' feet with the "water of the Word."

At a pastors' conference where Pastor Oyama was the speaker, 125 Filipino pastors drafted a manifesto "officially forgiving the Japanese nation for wartime brutalities" and inviting Oyama to return with his wife and three children to be resident missionaries at in the Philippines.

One by one Japanese went out as foreign missionaries. The plan, as Tadenuma explained, was to "send out our number one men as trailblazers. They must first prove successful in home missionary work by pioneering on virgin soil to plant a truly indigenous church which from the beginning will be a mission-minded church. Eventually that church will be the sending, supporting church for the missionary. Then before we send a missionary out we insist on a post-graduate, practical internship program at the Asian Institute of Missions (AIM). This is a strictly Oriental concept of discipline known as the father-son, teacher-disciple principle. Not until they pass these two processes will they be sent out. We want to make haste slowly, for our proverb says, 'Isogaba maware' 'In haste one goeth about in a circle.'"

So Japanese missionaries began entering open doors in Korea, Okinawa, the Philippines, Formosa, Hong Kong, New Guinea, Indonesia, Thailand, Malaya, India, Pakistan and the Middle East. And they still are. It was a strategy envisioned, developed, and executed by Kenny Joseph and his colleagues. As he noted, "This is only a part of Japan's missions' history. There is much to be celebrated from the past and in the present."

Besides the overseas missionary work, Kenny also worked with an incredible Japanese lady preacher named "Mother Morimoto" who has given succor and love to Tokyo's drunks for decades.

"After preaching in our church, I was asked to interpret for a reporter and a photographer from a daily newspaper who were going to do a story on Mother Morimoto and then pray and preach at her evening service," Kenny recalled. "I brought them to the beautiful, new, all-white, three-story chapel that the Lord led her to build by selling her little house and buying the land. To build, she also had to borrow $60,000. The seven beautiful stained glass windows, each worth $1,000, were donated by the artist who made them."

Kenny said that what made Mother Morimoto so amazing was the unusual place where this and her other church were located – in Sanya, the "secret" slum of Tokyo where 7,000 men lived, worked, got drunk, and slept in the streets on cardboard boxes. It is the area where the sign over the corner liquor store says, "We sell more liquor than any other place in the world."

"Thirteen years ago, while nursing her dying husband, raising five children, and going to seminary, she worked at night in this slum section," Kenny said. "After her husband died, she devoted all of her time to working here, preaching on Sunday and Wednesday and going around every night on patrol. She used a great big bowl with hot steaming noodles and plastic dishes to give some to each hungry man. Last winter, when it was cold, 250 drunken men died while sleeping after obeying the blinking vending machine which beckoned, 'buy me for 90 cents and I'll give you warmth' "After showing us the beautiful new church, Mother Morimoto invited us to have a special bowl of noodles she learned to cook in China. She speaks Chinese, Korean, a little English, Japanese, and a little German. The reason she speaks Chinese is because she was evacuated from Fukuoka, to Korea during the War. There she met and married a Chinese doctor. They came to Japan and here he died. (As a girl of four, Mrs. Morimoto accepted Christ at a Southern Baptist Church.) God has since given her a husband who is a great help in her work. He was once also a drunken bum, now delivered and born again. Thus he knows first hand about the problems of these men. He is also a needed protection for her as she works in this potentially dangerous area. When reporters asked what she had to show for thirteen years of labor there, she said, '800 drunks have been converted and 300 baptized.'

"All this in the worst section of town where few male ministers could last very long. Some Catholic priests from Europe and America have come and tried their best, but it has mainly become like Alcoholics Anonymous, which do not necessarily involve Christianity. Missions, missionaries, and Japanese pastors have tried, but most have thrown up their hands. Communist and radical students have tried to agitate this into a social class struggle. The yakuza, [Japanese Mafia] are there, too."

"You would have to see Mother Morimoto in action to find out what motivates her to leave a more comfortable life to get up every morning to sell cosmetics door to door to make enough money to pay the $1,000 monthly payments on the two churches. After this, on Sundays and Wednesdays, after having services in both churches, she and her husband and a bodyguard, take their portable kitchen on the back of a bike and ladle hot noodles and vegetables to all those they find along the way... drunk, lying on a cardboard box or huddled around a fire, one man, with no socks. Then her husband, walking behind the soup kitchen, reaches into a box of used clothes and passes them out as he sees fit to the most needy. Of course, the noodles and clothes are never sufficient."

Kenny said that Mother Morimoto was surely the "strongest man" among all the 9,000 pastors of Japan!

"Why does this godly, dedicated woman have to go around selling cosmetics to provide for this work?" he asked. "Because she has never learned that other Christians should be helping her. We are trying to teach her, but it isn't easy..." "We also plan to let the whiskey companies know what's going on, as they make it possible for these men to sleep on cardboard boxes as long as they can get another drink. They are addicts created by these companies which spend millions of dollars on beautiful art galleries or tennis matches or golf tournaments. They ought to spend their money cleaning up the vomit and helping rescue these men they've sent to within five inches of hell..." "But the bottom line is, as Mother Morimoto says, that so many of the 800 men who have made decisions for Christ, repented of their sins and invited Christ in, and received eternal life, after they get a hot meal and leave the Mission."

Comfortably situated with his large family in a seven-bedroom home in Oizumigakuen, with an office in nearby Ekoda, as the 1970's dawned, Kenny pressed on with his mission's work. Inspired by Japanese like Morimoto, who were tending to home fires, Kenny began to personally focus overseas to other parts of Asia. His mission was about to expand:

"I never held a meeting without being invited by Japanese Christian leaders," said Kenny. "I have been in twenty-five countries always holding meetings under the local invitations and sponsorship. I was also the international coordinator for the Asian Laymen's Christian Association (ALCA)."

It was a time of social unrest, and Kenny had also been a vocal member of several Christian-based anti-Communist groups which had worked hard to halt the spread of Marxism into Japan.

"The difficulty of competing with the communists was a major theme in Christian literature of the 1950s," noted historian Tim Shorrock, whose parents had been in Japan as missionaries. "According to *Missions at Work*, a handbook for missionaries I recently found on my parents' bookshelf, half the books on social science in Japanese bookstores were Marxist texts. 'There is great interest in reading the Bible,' the authors reported. 'It is certainly a best seller. But there is a strong rivalry between it and communist books. The people are weighing the relative merits of the two.' One chapter described a Communist-led labor demonstration ('a band of students, bewildered, seeking, young people') and asked if those 'lost souls' would follow the church or the 'Communist neighbor to the west, with their system of armed suppression in the name of peace and equality. 'Christianity is losing to Communism in the battle for Japan's youth, in the opinion of one American Protestant Missionary,' Kalisher reported in the lead to his story, as reprinted in the Japanese daily *Mainichi*. 'The Japanese church has no program to offer the thousands of young people searching and trying to grasp some sort of meaning for life,' Kalischer quoted my father as saying. 'It is regrettable that many non-Christians think that the only thing a Christian does is pray.' The church, he went on to say, 'is not challenging young people today. If anything, it is causing many young people to turn from Christianity, to fall headlong into an empty chasm of doubt and materialism, forcing them to join the Communist bandwagon, for at least the Communists have a program and a cause.' By the late 1940s, American political and military leaders concluded they were losing the battle for Asian hearts and minds, not only in Japan, but in Korea, China, and Southeast Asia as well. As tensions with the Soviet Union escalated in Europe and Mao Tse Tung's armies began chasing Chiang Kai Shek's nationalists out of China, the United States went on an offensive against what it considered the global forces of communism. Japan quickly became the linchpin for the U.S. Cold War strategy in the Far East. Conservative missionaries soon began to clash with the social reformers who came to Japan in the 1940s. Long before I ever heard the term "religious right," I was acutely aware of the deep conflicts between missionaries like my parents, who stressed the importance of social change and tolerance towards other religions, and those who insisted on a literal interpretation of the Bible and believed that anybody who wasn't saved was condemned to a life in hell. In the 1950s, I remember my father taking great pleasure in ridiculing the fundamentalist preachers, who came from churches with strange names like Far Eastern Gospel Crusade, The Navigators, and The New Tribes Mission, and drove around rural Japan in cars decorated with images of Jesus and the American flag, blending their evangelism with warlike sermons against the evils of communism. A decade later, the conflicts inside the missionary community between the social reformers and anti-communist evangelicals exploded over the Vietnam War: Liberals like my parents opposed U.S. involvement, while the fundamentalists supported it. Japanese Christian institutions were also ripped apart by struggles between conservatives and radicals opposed to the Vietnam War and American dominance of Japan."

Like so many Americans, Kenny Joseph watched in horror as the Vietnam War raged, bringing so much pain to the Vietnamese people when it was reported that the military on both sides suffered 1.1 million dead and 600,000 wounded during Hanoi's conflict with the United States. Civilian deaths were put at two million in the North and South. The Vietnam War also cost the United States 58,000 lives and 350,000 casualties.

Just before chaos broke out in Saigon, Kenny felt the Lord calling him to hold the last Christian outreach in the country before the Communists took over. He flew to Saigon and held a typical ALCA crusade – five days – morning and afternoons, with a small team of preachers and laymen teaching Christian leaders and then in the evening a crusade where the Gospel was preached. During the Saigon meetings, Kenny interpreted for Japan's Billy Graham: Evangelist Koji Honda.

"He would preach in Japanese, and I would translate it into English, and the Vietnamese interpreter interpreted to the people," he said. "Ten minutes became thirty minutes. At the invitation to receive Christ, over 600 came forward. It was literally Vietnam's last chance. The ALCA president was layman Tomezo Suzuki who planned to give $3,000 as an offering to Vietnam's layman's group. While shopping, he put his briefcase down, and a crippled orphan in a split second stole his purse that had in it the $3,000. Seeing him run away, I told the police and also American military police to get that money back. One of the Vietnamese who witnessed the theft said, 'We know who he is and he'll come out in three days. He is on drugs.' The police told us to wait for three days and they would keep $1,000 and give him $1,000 and return $1,000 to Suzuki. 'That's how it works.' Suzuki said, 'Keep it. We're leaving tomorrow.' Then into our room came a young Vietnam Air Force pilot. He said, 'You're going to leave for Tokyo tomorrow. Where do I go, with a wife and three children? We only get a third of the ammunition and bombs we need. We know we are sold out.' I said, 'I am from Chicago and if I wanted to cut my grass, I'd borrow my neighbor's lawn mower. You know how to fly the world's biggest plane, a C-130. You know that the pastors are on the first list for execution by the Atheist Communists. Borrow that plane and load it with all the pastors and families and baggage and take off for Guam – America's closest air base.' Can you believe it? He did...with seventy pastors and families and their baggage."

When he returned home, Kenny had tears in his eyes as he watched, the hysterical South Vietnamese officials and civilians scrambling to leave Saigon, on television. Martial law was declared. American helicopters began evacuating South Vietnamese, U.S., and foreign nationals from various parts of the city and from the U.S. embassy compound. Operation Frequent Wind had been delayed until the last possible moment because of U.S. Ambassador Graham Martin's belief that Saigon could be held and that a political settlement could be reached. Defense Secretary Schlesinger announced early on the morning of April 29th, 1975, the evacuation from Saigon by helicopter of the last U.S. diplomatic, military, and civilian personnel. Frequent Wind was arguably the largest helicopter evacuation in history. It began, in an atmosphere of desperation, as hysterical crowds of Vietnamese vied for limited seats. Martin pleaded with Washington to dispatch $700 million in emergency aid to bolster the regime and help it mobilize fresh military reserves. But American public opinion had soured on this conflict halfway around the world. In the U.S., South Vietnam was perceived as doomed. President Gerald Ford gave a televised speech on April 23rd, declaring an end to the Vietnam War and all U.S. aid. Frequent Wind continued around the clock, as North Vietnamese tanks breached defenses on the outskirts of Saigon. The song "White Christmas" was broadcast as the final signal for withdrawal. In the early morning hours of April 30th, the last U.S. Marines evacuated the embassy by helicopter, as civilians swamped the perimeter and poured onto the grounds. Many of them had been employed by the Americans and were left to their fate. On April 30th, 1975, VPA troops overcame all resistance, quickly capturing key buildings and installations. A tank crashed through the gates of the Presidential Palace, and at 11:30 a.m. local time, the NLF flag was raised above it. Thieu's successor, President Duong Van Minh, attempted to surrender, but VPA officers informed him that he had nothing left to surrender. Minh then issued his last command, ordering all South Vietnamese troops to lay down their arms.

The Communists had attained their goal: they had toppled the Saigon regime. But the cost of victory was high. In that past decade alone, one in ten Vietnamese had been a casualty of war – nearly a million and a half killed, three million wounded. Not wanting other Asian countries to fall like Vietnam, Kenny began visiting other threatened countries at the invitation of the Asian Christian Anti-Communist Association (ACALA), and they would do the same schedule. Kenny recalled when the flamboyant anti-communist crusader, Billy James Hargis of the Christian Crusade, attended and spoke at one of the events.

"One night at about 2 a.m. he called me and asked me to come and talk with him as he had heard the bombing and saw the flashes light and was scared," said Kenny. "I said, 'Come on! You are a Fearless Fosdick crusader. Remember that and go back to sleep.'"

(Fearless Fosdick made his Li'l Abner debut in a Sunday sequence in August of 1942, as the unflappable comic book idol of Abner's and, we are told, of all "red-blooded American boys." An object of undying hero worship, Li'l Abner mindlessly aped his role model – even once styling his hair similarly by using the product Fosdick endorsed.)

Kenny also loved to be involved in unique evangelistic opportunities. On one occasion, he helped send hot air balloons into China.

"As a member of ACACA laymen (Asian Christian Anti-Communist Association), we in Japan were especially close to South Korea and Taiwan," he said. "On one occasion, they flew us to Quemoy, a small island within sight of Mainland China. China would send over propaganda 'bombs' with rolled-up propaganda leaflets. In return, Taiwan would send over huge balloons in October when the wind was going toward China. We got permission to put in Chinese Gospel tracts on waterproof paper so that even if it rained they didn't disintegrate. These had a colored picture of Jesus knocking at the door of one's heart. Thousands landed in so many places that the police could not keep up with trying to catch them all, and we know many landed and were picked up by empty hearts. One testimony was from a pastor who baptized a believer in a bathtub. The project was called 'Love China.'"

Kenny always had a love for the huge land of India, and on one occasion, he was welcomed by Mar Thoma, the Patriarch of the Church of the East.

"He had me preach to 8,000 women on one side and men on the other and children up front," Kenny recalled. "I also worked with P.P. Job of the Asian Outreach. We linked up with an Operation Mobilization (OM) team of eleven Indians and one British PhD-turned-missionary. After we had showed the Jesus film, I began preaching through an interpreter and from behind the platform came plain-clothes police asking if I had any heroin. I motioned to my head saying my hair was very thin. 'No, I mean drugs,' he said. 'Heroin.' We found out later that he had captured several people on the beach and thought we might have been of that group."

## Indonesia

Another of Kenny's fascinations was Indonesia. With its 17,508 islands, it is the world's largest archipelagic state. With an estimated population of around 237 million people, it is the world's fourth most populous country and the most populous Muslim-majority nation.

So when he was invited to travel to Indonesia at Easter time some years back, Kenny was delighted with the opportunity to preach the Good News there.

"I was invited by one of Indonesia's young evangelists and Bible school president to come for evangelistic meetings in that country. Even though I suffer under Southeast Asia's oppressive no-breeze heat, I went," he joked.

"Teaching 500 Bible school students every morning through an interpreter using an overhead projector was a challenge. I preached at nightly meetings. It was so hot during the day that only a foreigner wears a tie even in formal meetings, so that was one relief. However on Sunday I had to wear one for their special Easter worship service. Driving to church, without air conditioning, we opened a window and put a wet wash cloth over our noses so as not to inhale the prevailing pollution. In Jakarta they use unemployed men as whistle-toting car 'parkers.' They help you back your car into a parking place, guard it, and then help you drive out. On the way out, you tip them about 300 rupees – 10 cents – or else!"

Kenny said that upon arrival at the church, he opened the car door and stepped out onto what he thought was solid ground, but soon discovered it was actually a "dastardly deep, dark, dirty ditch full of the garbage and filthy raw sewage of ten years' accumulation!"

He went on to say, "I immediately sank over my head into the slime, all the time grasping my bag that contained my Bible, camera, tape recorder and other important items. Bobbing up and down, I managed to latch one hand onto the side of the pit and pull myself up. I was greeted by laughter, shock, and horror from the bystanders who saw all this! The 'parker' was clearly embarrassed and ran for hiding. The pastor said, 'Why didn't you watch your step?'"

Kenny said that fortunately he had put most of his personal belongings into Zip-Lock plastic bags to protect them from the humidity. As he sloshed his way to the church, only 300 feet away, instead of being angry, he started to sing and praise God, counting his blessings, thinking, "Well, this could have happened out in the country where I wouldn't be near a church which has a 'bathroom' (where you take a bath using a little dipper of cold water and wash outside the tub of standing water, never getting in)." What did he sing? Snatches from…

*I serve a risen Savior, He's In the world today;*
*I know that He is living, whatever men may say;*
*I see His hand of mercy, I hear His voice of cheer,*
*And just the time I need Him, He's always near. He lives, He lives,*
*Christ Jesus lives today!*
*He walks with me and talks with me*
*Along life's narrow way. He lives, He lives, salvation to impart!*
*You ask me how I know He lives?*
*He lives within my heart! In all the world around me I see His loving care,*
*Tho' my heart grows weary, I never will despair;*
*I know that He is leading, thro' the stormy blast,*
*The day of His appearing will come at last. Rejoice, rejoice, O Christian,*
*Lift up your voice and sing*
*Eternal hallelujahs to Jesus Christ the King!*
*The hope of all who seek Him,*
*The help of all who find,*
*None other is so loving, so good and kind.*

"I thought to myself, this dirty black gooey sewage that I washed off was only one-billionth of the 'garbage' Jesus bore on the cross for our sins," Kenny recalled. "As I came out of that bathroom all washed up I felt like I had returned from hell and the grave and was purged so I sang, 'And sinner plunged beneath that flood... Lose all their guilty stains.' Since the pastor was at least 50 pounds lighter than me, where could I find adequate clothes in time for the Easter morning service that by now had already begun? Fortunately the pastor's wife was a seamstress."

Kenny said that she led him to her treasure trove of unclaimed clothes, and after trying on several pairs of pants, he found one that fit, a loud "Indonesian batik," a beautiful, hand-made colorful shirt worn by all Indonesians, even their President, on formal occasions.

So Kenny Joseph made a quick recovery and was soon up and was clean and ready.

"And so, there I was sitting on a chair on a platform of the church squeaky clean," he recalled. "After the pastor spoke for a while everyone suddenly burst out laughing! He had explained in detail what had happened! Big joke! It was also the most receptive audience I've had in years. I gave them the Bible's basic Good News that Saint Paul gave all those years ago in 1 Corinthians 15:1-4."

> 1. Now let me remind you (since it seems to have escaped you) of the Gospel - the glad tidings of salvation - which I proclaimed to you, which you welcomed and accepted and upon which your faith rests;
> 2. And by which you are saved, if you hold fast and keep firmly what I preached to you, unless you believed at first without effect and all for nothing.
> 3. For I passed on to you what I also received: that Christ the Messiah, the Anointed one, died for our sins.
> 4. That He was buried and that He arose and on the third day as the Scriptures foretold...

Kenny then gave the invitation for people to come forward, and many seekers streamed forward to kneel and receive God's blessings with both outstretched hands in prayer lifted up as cups while the congregation sang praises to God:

> *"Fill my cup Lord I lift it up Lord;*
> *Come and lift this longing in my soul'*
> *Bread of Heaven feed me till I want no more*
> *Fill my cup, fill it up and make me whole"*

Kenny said that the interpreter devised a way to combine three invitations into one. He shouted, "Everyone who wants to be born again, saved, on the right. Everyone who wants to rededicate and consecrate themselves in the middle. Those who want to be filled with the Holy Spirit for power and service to the left. Anyone who wants healing to the far left."

Kenny stood watching in fascination, having sung and preached for an hour.

"Yet I had to go around and personally lay my hands on a hundred sweating peoples' heads wearing the white gloves graciously provided for me," he said. "Many received the blessing they sought that day." He went on to say, "After returning to Tokyo, I was so grateful for cool breezes that I forgot about an unhealed cut on my arm. I finally asked a nurse who had served in Indonesia about it. She said, 'Yes, that's a bacteria infection from that garbage drain. I've known Indonesians whose body bloated up, others went blind. Your recovery was fast because of your good health. It's good you didn't open your eyes in that pit!'"

Kenny said he will never forget his Easter in Indonesia, adding, "I rose up from that slimy pit to a victorious Easter service. We all can rise from the slimy pit of this world's sin to new life by believing in the crucified, risen Christ... and then to be eternally resurrected to Heaven with the resurrected Christ. He's alive and waiting for us! All because He Lives.

*"Because He lives I can face tomorrow;*
*"Because He lives all fear is gone;*
*"Because I know He holds the future,*
*"And life is worth the living Just because He lives"*

## Iraq

Another land where Kenny's ministry extended to was Iraq, where he has traveled to several times.

He began to see reports that "many churches and seminaries [were] being bombed just as the people were leaving church... History is repeating itself, and the only thing we learn from history is that we learn nothing from history. To behead a Christian in Allah's name is a sin."

Joseph said that he promised his mother before she passed away that he would set up the "Martha Joseph Memorial Bible Campaign."

"I was invited to start a new Bible Land Tour going through Iraq's Garden of Eden, Ur, Babylon, Baghdad, Nineveh, and then on to the seven churches spoken of in the book of Revelation in the Bible, and then to come down on the Damascus Road where Jewish Paul was converted in Syria," he recalled. "We helped get in 14,000 Bibles as long as they were kept inside of churches."

Today, Kenny's work in Iraq continues through his son Ken who travels there frequently to minister to the Iraqi people.

# Chapter 10

## *Trouble and Transformation*

By the mid 1970s Kenny and Lila Joseph were successful missionaries in a difficult to work field, with four growing and healthy children. From all outward appearances, they were the picture perfect missionary couple. But below the surface, a problem was haunting Kenny that would soon come to head in a dramatic way.

Just as life was settling down for Kenny and Lila in Japan, a huge problem arose when a lawsuit was brought against Kenny over the mission property. A differing understanding of the transaction led Kenny to think that he would be allowed to continue to operate on the second floor of the building while the new owner occupied the first floor, that the new owner could remain a missionary with REAP's sister mission in Japan which Kenny had started, the Zenkoku Kirisuto Kyo Dendo-Kai (NCEA), and that over a period of ten years, ownership of the building would move to that owner, Mr. Kikuchi, a Japanese pastor, so long as he remained a member of the mission. Pastor Kikuchi, however, disputed that understanding and sued Kenny in Japanese court for breach of contract. As the court case dragged on, Kenny and Lila's reputation would be damaged amidst the tight-knit missionary community in Japan and cause marital strains within the Joseph family. In the summer of 1976, Lila abruptly returned to the U.S. with her eight year-old son Mark for consultations with board members of the mission, who urged Kenny to settle the lawsuit even if it meant taking a loss. After much soul-searching and considerable pain, Kenny did so, accepting a lump sum payment. He vacated the offices he had built at Ekoda and moved his offices to the Joseph home in Oizumigakuen.

But the stress of fighting the legal battle would take its toll, and when Kenny and Lila returned to the United States with their family in 1977, they weren't even sure if they'd ever be returning to Japan. Settling in La Mirada, California to be near their sons Bobb and Kimbo who were attending Biola College, the Joseph family purchased a home and kept themselves busy by physically fixing up the property. They even won an award from the city for being the most improved home in the community.

"Today I drive by the house and I remember how it used to look when we first bought it and began work on the ultimate fixer-upper," remembered Mark who was nine years old at the time. "Together, my three brothers and our parents worked to make the old house habitable. It was 1977 before land prices skyrocketed in California, but even by those standards, our purchase of a four-bedroom house with a pool and a large backyard complete with fruit trees for $69,000 was a steal. There was one catch: The house was a dump. As we surveyed the backyard, it was obvious the property had been abandoned. Large, ominous weeds growing in many directions made walking difficult. The pool was cracked, the kitchen tile unusable, and the wall was covered with layers of wallpaper. In short, the house was a mess. None of us probably realized it at the time, consciously anyway, but it was a lot like our family. We too were a mess. The summer before I had been wrenched away from home by my Mother and brothers, who had planned an escape that would keep Mom and I away from the rest of the family for the entire summer. Life at home had become an endless series of arguments and problems, and somehow it had been decided by people with minds far above my own 8-year old one that this was the solution.

"Our family issues then were complex, involving marital difficulties, a lawsuit, a mission, betrayal, a rocky eldest son-father relationship, paranoia, a lack of communication, and complex spiritual problems – complicated stuff. Knocking out windows, fixing wallpaper, and cutting weeds was tough labor, but it was tangible and easy to get at, unlike the deep-seated problems in our family.

"We threw ourselves into the task of rebuilding that house. There was much to be done, and each of us did our part. My eldest brother was sure that the upstairs window had to be enlarged and happily set to work. Another brother removed the multiple layers of wallpaper, and when he got tired, used the enlarged window to launch himself into the pool thirty feet below. Still another brother worked on the yard—making sure the trees were pruned and the grass planted. My Mother supervised the kitchen repairs, adding touches of harvest gold wherever she could and planting flowers in what was once an overgrown front yard. Dad and I went to the local home supply store to buy the materials to construct a basketball hoop on our new garage. Somehow our family, once on the verge of breaking up, came together through the process of repairing the old house. We had found a way to set aside our problems and attack a common enemy – the ugly house – and months later as we marveled at our work, we never stopped to notice that God was repairing our family just as he had allowed us to repair the old house.

"Gradually our family life began to mimic the transformation that had come over our house. On Sundays we enjoyed having dinner in the back yard with different guests each week. We spent many hours in the pool we had lovingly reconstructed, and enjoyed Christmases and Thanksgivings in the dining room that had once been unlivable. As I drive by that home today and slow down to take a peek inside just to see how the new occupants are keeping up the place, I notice that the front lawn is manicured, and the house has gotten a new coat of paint, but I still remember it the way it was before God used twelve loving hands to breathe new life into it. And I remember also how God himself breathed life into our family, giving us new hope and strength to carry on, and ride out the storms of life together."

The transformation Mark described had occurred as a result of a life-altering experience that Kenny had while on furlough in the U.S., when he finally came to grips with a problem that had slowly been destroying him and had what he would later call his "Wainwright Experience."

"I was under serious spiritual oppression and though others around me were aware of it, I was not," Kenny recalled. "I was in a bubble. Everybody else was wrong and I was right. My prayers felt as though they were bouncing off of the ceiling, and the Bible was a dead book to me. As I was seeking the Lord from the bottom of this acute depression, the June 1978 Herald of His Coming magazine came into my hands. I had considered it a boring magazine, but this is the one thing God used to get to me."

The magazine had no pictures, just articles, but then a story about a World War II general, General Wainwright caught his eye.

"The article talked about a book, Forever Triumphant, by F.J. Huegel which told a story that came out of World War II," Kenny recalled. "After General Wainwright was captured by the Japanese, he was held a prisoner in a Manchurian concentration camp. Japanese prison keepers made him an object of their mockery day by day. He knew nothing of what was happening in the outside world. He became a skeleton, as it were, a broken, crushed, hopeless, starving man. Finally the Japanese surrendered, and the war ended. One day an airplane landed in the camp, and a colonel of the Allied forces marched up to General Wainwright telling him that Japan had been defeated. Imagine the effect of such news upon the spirit of this dying man. The colonel, having delivered his message, took to the skies once more. When Japanese prison keepers, not knowing what had happened, returned to mock and buffet the General as formerly he declared with authority, 'No, I am in command here! These are my orders.' F.J. Huegel observed that from that moment on, General Wainwright was in control. Huegel made this application: "Have you been informed of the victory of your Savior – in the greatest conflict of the ages? Have you heard his voice, 'Behold, I give unto you power...over all the power of the enemy?' (Luke 10:19). Then rise up to assert your rights. You are now a king. Rise up to reign. Give the command of faith. Never again go under – when the enemy comes to oppress. Say with firmness, 'I am in command here.' Give your orders, in the name of the Lord, and by His authority and through His power. The enemy, thus resisted will flee (James 4:6-8), and you will live and work victoriously no matter how many or in what manner the demons come against you. Claim the victory in Jesus' Name. We must learn to stand on resurrection ground, reckoning dead the old-creation life over which Satan has power, and living in the new creation, over which Satan has no power whatever.'

For Kenny, the transformation was instantaneous. "I sensed the Lord saying to me, 'Stand up, Kenny. You are in charge. Tell those evil spirits that are bugging you to leave!' I started calling out their names and got so loud that Lila told me to 'calm down' or 'the neighbors would hear me!' I came in to the room where Lila went back into, and I asked her to grab a pad to write down in shorthand what I was saying – 'anger, hatred, lying, fear, out in the Name of Jesus.' The list went on and on. As I stood before the Lord and my wife, we called out in the Name of Jesus 23 oppressing, depressing, obsessing spirits, attitudes, and traits. We commanded them to leave in the Name of Jesus and never return: hate, fear, rejection, rebellion, lust, lying, deceit, stealing, sarcasm, criticism, divisiveness, doubt, down spirit, heaviness, dark, blind, depressive, paranoia, anger, mad, not giving love and touchy. We also invited the 23 opposite traits of the Holy Spirit: love, trust, acceptance, submission, truth, honesty, restoring, compliment, praise, unity, faith, up, lighthearted, bright, light, sight, positive, optimistic, whole, happy, giving love and calm. I received a great deliverance, freedom, and a new sense of being in charge of myself. Not really me, but the Holy Spirit. After that I felt I had holes over my body as the evil spirits left. And then I wondered how I could fill those holes, so I called in opposites – 'quietness, love, truthfulness and peace.' Our two sons, Ken and Bobby, were attending Biola University, and there was a professor there named Dr. Murphy who then came and spent time with us, helping us understand this binding of 'generational curses', which made me immediately concerned for my personal family since we may have had some generational binding. He was very wise in treading this often-unknown and untaught path and helped me a great deal to begin walking a new path."

Kenny's first order of business was to extend apologies to those whom God brought to his mind. "I immediately realized how many had been stumbled by my life," he said. "I went to each of my boys, taking them separately out to a meal, and gave my testimony and asked them to forgive me and help me. Each one was happy to respond favorably for both problems. Then I, alone, flew back to Japan and went to each one that I felt had something against me or that I knew I had hurt. With tears I asked each one to forgive me, and with tears of joy we were reconciled. The key was the principle taught at the Bill Gothard Institute of Basic Youth Conflicts. Just a few words: I realize I was wrong in... Will you forgive me? Always as a question. The ball is then on the other side and he must answer yes or no. If yes, it's over. If no, it's his problem. As we traveled across America on this furlough, I often shared this personal testimony even though it was sometimes hard. But I couldn't dwell on what the listeners would think; just that I knew what the Lord had done for me, and hopefully some contacts listeners also needed similar deliverance."

For Kenny's second son Bobb, the Wainwright experience marked a defining threshold in his relationship with his parents. "Like most parents, they were stricter in the early days and loosened up later on," he says. "We got the 'belt' from Dad or a spanking from Mom sometimes when we disobeyed or did something wrong. [But the] biggest change was when Dad had his 'Wainwright' experience not long after I graduated from high school. He was a broken man, and asked for forgiveness for not being the best father, and for any way he may have wronged each of us. It was a real example of the regenerative work of the Holy Spirit, and an encouragement to me to maintain a forgiving relationship with others. Also, both Mom and Dad have 'softened' in a positive way in their theological approaches. While they (particularly Dad) were fairly strict fundamentalist early on, they became more tolerant of, for example, Charismatic and non-fundamentalist groups and churches. Part of this may have been due to my older brother, Kimbo, and his embracing of the Charismatic Movement with his involvement with Calvary Chapel in the late '70s. Mom and Dad also attended a Friends Church in California while on furlough in 1977-1978."

On Sunday evenings, they sometimes attended a Charismatic church, Melodyland Christian Center, close to Disneyland in Anaheim, California. Bobb adds, "How I view Dad has changed somewhat over the years. Part of this is the 'BW' and 'AW' ('Before Wainwright' and 'After Wainwright'). He could sometimes be harsh with me when I was younger (e.g., I wished he would say 'please' and 'thank you' more; he would call me a 'baby girl' or 'are you afraid of your shadow' if I didn't do something that I didn't feel ready to do), but I always knew that he loved me. And he would express it in non-verbal ways that I understood and took to heart. Although he didn't always verbalize his love, little notes he would write from Evangelistic trips, drawings he would make, or things he would do – like reading to me, getting me an ice cream cone, taking me on trips with him, told me so."

For Kenny's youngest son Mark, the change was dramatic. Kenny asked each of his sons out to a restaurant individually and asked for the forgiveness of each:

"We settled into a booth at our neighborhood IHOP," Mark remembered. "I leapt at the chance which didn't come often to this ten-year old. He began by telling me he'd been a lousy Dad – which wasn't news to me. He told me that he'd had an encounter with God that has freed him from the compulsions to control and bully or something to that effect. The combination of a spiritual counselor/exorcist who helped identify the spirits that were tormenting him and an old World War II story he read had caused him to rethink his life, and he'd received strength and revelation from God in a new way that had brought us to IHOP today. That day I was proud of him in a way that I hadn't been. He showed me how to be a man."

Spiritually reinvigorated and ready to serve again, Kenny, Lila, Jim, and Mark returned to Japan in the summer of 1979, and the entire family began a new chapter in their lives and in Kenny and Lila's ministry as a new friend of Kenny's, William F. Turner helped organize a new board for the mission. As Mark enrolled in the sixth grade at the Christian Academy in Japan and Jim in the 12th grade, Kenny began new pathways of ministry even as he continued previous responsibilities such as pastoring the church that met at their home. As usual, Kenny's flexible schedule and readiness to move in any direction God called him allowed him to be involved with a number of outreach efforts. During this period of time, one involved ministering to Iranians who were living in Japan:

"There were six thousand Iranians who gathered at Yoyogi Park in Tokyo every Sunday," he recalled. Kenny was challenged by a phone call from an evangelist passing through Narita Airport to do something about this incredible opportunity. "We printed 40,000 Iranian tracts (Four Things God Wants You to Know) with the word 'Allah' (God) on the front. Not one was thrown away be cause as Salem Kamel said, 'You can't put "God" on the dirty ground.' On the back we printed a railway subway map. As we passed out these tracts, we were sometimes mobbed, and they were taken like hotcakes. We told everyone to go down the street and find a white church where there would be music and a message. Up to twenty went, looking over their shoulders to check who might be watching."

Sending son Jim off to college in 1980, Kenny & Lila settled in for a six-year stretch of life on the mission field that would see their youngest son Mark go from a chubby seventh grader to a senior in high school, graduating in 1986 and ready to return to the U.S. for college. Kenny and Lila and Mark returned that summer as Mark settled into college at Biola University, and Kenny & Lila began a motor home trip across the U.S to meet with their supporters. After a year in the U.S., in the fall of 1987, Kenny & Lila would return to Japan as empty-nesters with their children across the U.S.

Kenny was also about to discover a whole new avenue of ministry: weddings. When he returned to Japan in 1987, his ministry took a surprising turn when he began officiating at weddings in Tokyo. At this time he was on one of the 20 planning committees, comprised of 100 pastors, for the Tokyo crusade featuring Evangelist Koji Honda. The crusade was held at a hall in the Aogaku Kaikan in Tokyo and had 600 attendees, 500 who were already Christians. So their year of hard work got 100 new people to hear the Gospel message.

"At the same time I heard things about the 'Christian' wedding business, with big mission leaders saying it was a 'racket,'" he recalled. "To make money teaching English was 'pure.' To make money having weddings was 'unclean.' So I parroted that line, too, until someone said, 'Don't knock it 'til you try it.' So I said, 'OK, I'll try it and then knock it. I was asked to preach at six weddings at a wedding hall in Tokyo... one every half hour. I was unaccustomed to it, so I got out my Missionary Language Handbook and turned to the wedding section and read it. But halfway through, it dawned on me that here were 100 unsaved people who had never been to a Christian church before. This was their first impression of Christianity. So the next wedding, I took them back to the first wedding in the Garden of Eden and introduced God and His Son, the only way, truth and life and that no one could come to the Father but through Jesus. I took them to the cross where Christ died for their sins, sacrificed His life for us as the husband must do for his wife, and then I had Jesus rising from the dead in the triumph of love. I preached to the 80 people over the heads of this couple. I got warmed up by the sixth one, and then as I as walking home I thought, 'I would pay money to do this, and here they pay me an honorarium.'

"I thought back on how a hundred preachers huffed and puffed for a year to get out a total of 100 unsaved people at the cost of three million yen. To get 500 unsaved people out on a Sunday would take 10 million yen of advertising. So I decided this was a good way to open Japan's hearts: through weddings. At Nihon Kaku, Japan's oldest wedding hall, there were no Christian weddings before and after the War, but now it's up to 35%, chosen by the bride-to-be, sometimes against her Shinto parents' wishes. This is what one missionary calls 'a very effective evangelistic opening.' A Southern Baptist missionary said, "This is the mass evangelism method in Japan today."

Always looking for new ways to present the Gospel to the Japanese, Kenny next turned his attention to graphic novels, working with a nationally known artist named Madoka to create a graphic novel that illustrated the True Love Waits campaign encouraging Japanese young people to rethink their attitudes toward sexuality. Another series illustrated Kenny's work on the origins of Christianity in Japan.

"We made a new top ten overhead projector transparency series," he said. "We weren't copying David Letterman, but Almighty God and His Ten Commandments. We compared it to a bicycle wheel with ten spokes, but they all go to the center of the wheel, which is Christ. After two years of work, we had 25 messages for Christians and 25 for non-believers. Each one had an index and ten colored illustrations. At the same time, the artist illustrated our bilingual book of the Nestorian Missionary Movement. This book was first called 'Jizo and Jesus,' Jizo being the Buddhist guardian angel of children in hell. The new name is now 'Japan's Christian Roots.' It has been morphed into Japanese only and called 'The Country of the Erased Cross' which has sold over 20,000 copies in secular bookstores. The bestseller in Christian circles would be two or three thousand.

Now it has come out in a small paperback for half price to all the 14,000 bookstores. There are only 55 Christian stores, and my son, Ken Jr., and I get invited to speak at groups who've read it."

The Kenny Joseph of old was back in harness and loving every minute of it.

# Chapter 11

# *Life in The Land of The Rising Sun*

"Mournful ambulances and clanging fire engines," described Lila. "These are common sounds in a huge city like Tokyo with its more than 11 million people. Sickness and tragedy strike often. More cheerful and welcome events are made known in other ways." The Josephs learned much from Japanese culture, experiencing a whole new world – including the sounds of the city. Lila wrote:

"A cozy sound heard about October – that lasts through March – is the minor key of the man who goes through the neighborhood calling, 'Baked sweet potatoes for sale.' He either pulls his cart or sits on a powered one. It has a stove, complete with a smoking stovepipe, where rocks are kept hot. Into these hot rocks he keeps putting sweet potatoes, shuffling them around so they get baked. Then he's ready to sell them to hungry passers-by, young and old alike, after weighing them on a little hand scale. Another sound is the periodic clapping of two small slabs of wood is a sound relegated to cold, crisp winter evenings. Neighbors take turns at this job. The clapping is a specific warning: 'Be careful of fires! Be careful of fires!' Fires are especially feared where wooden houses are so close together.

"To find out the reason for the long, drawn-out, cheery, periodic bugle call in the air, you look for a man on a bicycle. He has a big wooden box on back and his call draws housewives from their homes all along his route. For them he stops, opens the lid, and brings out tofu for sale. Each piece is about the shape of a half a pound of butter. It's made of bean curd and is almost pure protein. Tofu can be prepared in many different ways.

Not to be forgotten is the man who drives up and down small streets in a truck announcing that he will trade bathroom tissue for your newspapers. And one garbage collector's loudspeaker boomed out the music of 'Shall We Gather at the River.'

Lila drew a spiritual application from the sounds:

"The Bible has something to say about sounds, too, one of which is, "If the trumpet gives forth an uncertain sound, who shall prepare himself...?" In other words, if we who claim to be Christians don't live like we should, who will we influence or help to realize the wonderful, happy sounds of salvation?"

One of the cultural differences she experienced was the differing approach to marriage. Though many young people in Japan have adopted Western ideas about love and marriage, many still prefer to have their mates chosen for them. In fact, until World War II, marriages chosen from romantic love were almost unheard of.

"I only saw my husband once before the ceremony, and then I was too bashful to really look at him," a lady once confided to Lila.

"This was not an isolated case, but just the way it was done in old-time Japan," observed Lila. "Today's matchmaking has been modernized. Naturally, the matchmaker is a very important person. Not just anybody cares to be responsible for a marriage. It just might not work out, and he would be to blame. So this is taken as a serious job. After all, the future of two young people is at stake. And two families are seriously involved. A matchmaker is called a 'nakodo.' Actually, a 'middle person.' A go-between. He is usually selected by the parents of one eligible party. Sometimes this is a couple, and if so, the wisdom of both husband and wife is combined. A matchmaker's first job is to get a picture and history of his 'client' and then set out to find a suitable partner. Family backgrounds, educational factors, character, hobbies and work are thoroughly looked into for both sides. When a likely couple emerges, each is given a picture and resume of the other person. A date is set for them to meet. One or both, in today's culture, may reject the choice. If agreeable, however, they begin dating, and eventually an engagement party with elaborate gifts follows. In all this, as well as in the up-coming wedding, the matchmaker is very active. "One man, Mr. Ishizaka, was a professional matchmaker for 45 years. Now in his seventies, he claims to have arranged some 3,000 weddings, and boasts that only five ended in divorce. Ishizaka began as a traveling salesman, but as he moved about the Islands, he was often asked to find a suitable partner for someone. Thus began a professional career in which he has few peers. It also highly qualifies him to speak about Asian marriages. One secret of arranging a good wedding, according to Mr. Ishizaka, is 'total honesty.' One partner should not be overly played up. And also, though a man may be poor, he must not be shrugged off. According to this experienced matchmaker, girls tend to want a man with good scholastic standing, while a man looks for beauty. Japanese believe that love will develop after the wedding. Before the war, Mr. Ishizaka traveled as far as Singapore, China and Taiwan, and after the War even to New York to arrange marriages. And he's still on the lookout for partners today. He carries personal records and photographs of more than 300 prospective partners."

## The Bonsai

Known around the world for its fine gardens, the Japanese bonsai plant, provided inspiration for Lila. "The beautifully shaped pine trees were only about 2 ½ to 3 feet high," she wrote. "Still they were fully grown. In fact, the gardener told us, they were about 150 years old. These were 'bonsai' (bone-sah-ee) – the stunted trees. And this was a bonsai garden: a well-groomed, attractive shop on the guided bus tour.

"Bonsai are peculiar to the Orient. Growing them may be a hobby or a business. But no matter that, it's an art requiring skilled hands, much care, and lots of patience. Not only is it a continual task to keep the plant alive, but at the same time the plant's growth must be guided and it's branches shaped to conform to set patterns. "The process of making a bonsai begins when the chosen plant is a baby. It is then planted into a small pot, which in time actually cramps the roots. It is given only enough water and fertilizer to keep it alive. At times strings and wires are used to tie branches, holding them down while guiding them into the desired shape. These are then taken off when the growing process is finished. Expert cutting and pruning are required. Effort is made to respect the natural tendency of growth while also guiding the plant's shape. Some bonsai plants are loaded with blossoms, while others bear fruit that can be eaten. But pine trees are the most common. Heights vary from a mere six inches to three feet tall. "Dwarfed potted plants date back over 800 years. Many books are available to the interested person, and beautiful specimens can be seen in many yards as you go for and afternoon stroll through Tokyo. One gardener was offered $10,000 for a 150-year-old pine bonsai. "Though recognizing the beauty of a bonsai, and not being insensitive to the skill required to grow one (mine died!), I still feel a little sad about this miniature specimen. Each one could have been a tall, handsome tree towing high in the breeze in somebody's yard. But it was purposely stunted, mainly from lack of nourishment. "It's like us humans sometimes. We may be full-grown, many years old, but actually shriveled up inside. We may think nobody knows. But what's on the inside is bound to show up in daily life. It's the inner person who guides the outer. A miserable personality full of self-pity and selfishness and grumpiness needs to have the strings cut and is set free. Jesus can do that. And as we read His Word, we get the nourishment we need for the stunted inner man to grow into a beautiful whole person."

## New Years

New Year's Day was always a big celebration in Japan. "Every year on December 31$^{st}$ at eleven-thirty, temple gongs begin to echo eerily, ominously through the quietness," remembered Lila. "Each gong sounds like when a piano note is held with your foot on the pedal. This is ushering in a new year, Oriental style. It is believed that man has 108 sins that have to be forgiven before he enters it. So 108 gongs sound. "New Year's time provides the longest vacation and is really the focal point of the year. It's a time of family reunions, causing trains and buses to be booked well in advance and to be very crowded. Tokyo-ites, especially, throng back to their country relatives. "Young people love to receive "otoshi-dama" (New Year's coins) at this time. This is simply a gift of money put into a colorful envelope especially bought for the occasion. Lots of doting relatives means a good number of fat money envelopes. "Before this, however, is much preparation. Homes and yards are thoroughly cleaned. Even the man of the house pitches in and helps wash windows and clean up. Special foods are prepared and enough to last for many days. From 15 to 30 different kinds of food are served on New Year's Day. These foods usually don't require refrigeration and are laid out artistically on lacquered trays that fit one upon another in a neat stack. The lady of the house must be sure to shop thoroughly because most stores are closed for at least four days into the New Year. As much as possible, debts are paid. In olden days, some who couldn't comply with that committed suicide. "My first year in Tokyo, we were away from home for a few days and arrived back on December 31$^{st}$. I was surprised to be greeted by a small line-up outside my door. At that time we paid our bills by the month, and the milkman, the meat man, the vegetable man and others wanted their pay before December ended. Great emphasis is placed on beginning the New Year with a clean slate. "Often we would love to begin again. 'If I could live over my life that is past,' the songwriter wrote. Sad to say, just flipping the calendar or making New Year's resolutions doesn't change us. But the Bible has a solution: 'If any man be in Christ, he is a new creature. Old things are passed away, all things are become new.'"

## The Heist

Another memory of life in Japan for Lila was being there during a criminal heist and drawing illustrations from it. "Almost 3 million yen (now $30,000) is what he drove off with," recalled Lila. "The mastermind of the most celebrated crime in Japan's postwar history, that is. And what's more, the statute of limitations was up on December 9th, 1975 – at midnight. Not only is he now immune to any criminal penalties (though he must give back the money if caught), but he has become somewhat of a hero. "Rolling through the outskirts of Tokyo on the morning of December 10th, 1968, was a car with a driver, three guards, and nearly $30,000 in cash. The money car, from a nearby bank, was taking the cash to pay employees of an electrical manufacturing plant their year-end bonuses. Suddenly a man dressed like a policeman, and riding the typical white motorcycle, stopped them. There might be a bomb in or under the car, he warned them. While they scurried to safer quarters, smoke did really begin to pour from the car – from a canister he deftly planted. With the coast clear, the 'policeman' jumped in the car and drove off, taking the $30,000. He's never been found and neither has the money.

"Seven years of intensive investigation has cost many times the amount of the loot. Some 171,520 man-days of police and detective manpower worked on tracking down clues that led nowhere. Police got 28,042 tips, and they paid $30 reward, for any that seemed worthwhile. They cleared 110,000 suspects.

Plenty of clues were left–the motorcycle and two getaway cars, all stolen, were found. The smoke canister and three footlockers that held the cash were abandoned. So were the gimmicks on the motorcycle to make it look like a police vehicle. There was even an eyewitness description that police used to reconstruct a picture for the public. He is the "best-known unknown" in Japan, one newspaper said.

"Tremendous public interest surrounded this crime, right down to the midnight countdown of the statute of limitations. Young people actually hoped the robber wouldn't be caught. He used no weapons... nobody was killed or even hurt, they reasoned. Not only was his actual act bold and imaginative, but his continued evasion of the law has proven his wit. One newspaper chided police for mistakes in their investigation, but also scolded the public for the 'hero' image accorded this criminal.

"One thing this smart robber hasn't reckoned with, though: 'Thou God seest me.' And He sees you and me. We're clearly told that we'll all stand before God to give an account of the things we did down here. It's a wise person who starts getting acquainted now with the only Person Who can help us then: Jesus Christ."

## Lost & Found

As Americans living on the other side of the world, the Josephs and their friends and family had some close calls. "How we searched for Julia's ticket and passport!" said Lila, remembering the time a child's documents were misplaced. "Somehow they hadn't been put into the locked security box where we usually put important papers and documents. The three kids who were here from America and us gathered together and prayed. And we searched. Every possible place, we thought. Finally we called Julia's parents in California. Her father said, "Remember when I was there I gave them to you one evening before bedtime. But don't worry. We can get a new passport and replace the ticket." But that would take many days and leave Julia (then age seven) here alone while her brother and his friend (both nine) went on ahead home. I went to make another telephone call and was absentmindedly shuffling through some papers that had collected by the telephone. Imagine my feelings when... there were Julia's important items! Did we ever have a praise service! That was a firsthand lesson for those three children of God's intervention. I hope they never forget it!"

In a similar situation, Lila lost her own wallet once.

"One day I had been to the bank and taken out some money, come home, and suddenly I couldn't find my wallet," she remembered. "A friend was here helping me and we prayed together. Then we searched some more. Finally she said she felt I should go to the police about this loss. I went, but not before I had checked at the bank to be sure it wasn't there. It wasn't. So I headed for the nearby police station. One of the policemen on duty had me sit down in front of him and he wrote down the answers I gave to his questions about what was in my wallet. Okay. There were credit cards, some cash. But when I said that my Alien Registration card and my Japanese driver's license were also included, he looked up at me as if to say, 'Boy, are you in trouble!'

"When we finished, I headed home. It was dusk. Kenny was away somewhere. Marjie and I talked a little and she asked me what my wallet looked like. I told her. Then she took me to our pantry, pointed to a shelf, and said, 'Is this it?' There on the shelf was my precious wallet! I had laid it down there while getting out the vacuum cleaner. How we rejoiced and praised the Lord. Then I hurried to the police station, and I think the policeman was as happy as I was when he heard the good news. He hadn't had a chance to cancel my credit cards yet, so he said there would be no record of my police escapade!"

## Home Leaves

Missionary work also involved giving presentations back in the States. One time, Lila got to show the boys her old home during furlough.

"I remember once on home leave as we traveled across Montana that I told my boys to look good in all directions as they'd never see this sight in Tokyo... not a house, building or barn in any direction as far as you could see."

Another time, the family was in Texas where they were scheduled to have a missionary meeting. "As per directions," writes Lila, "we drove into the huge yard of the church to get hooked up for electricity. Kenny went inside to get pertinent information. As I waited in our motor home, a gentleman came to talk with me. 'Are you planning to stay here tonight?' he asked. When I assured him that we were, he said, 'Then I will bring you a gun.' I nearly had a heart attack. 'A gun? Why?' I blurted out. With a swoop of his arm over the church yard he explained, 'Look, if somebody should come to cause trouble, nobody would hear you call.' (Cell phones? Not back then!) Tom said that we should talk it over and decide what we wanted to do by the time he got back from driving somebody home. He added, 'You can park your motor home in our driveway.'

"Well, when Kenny came back, it didn't take us long to decide that we didn't want to stay where we were. So we happily accepted Tom's invitation and followed him to their home and parked in their driveway for the couple of days we were in the area. Tom and Gail have been dear friends of ours ever since. Gail is very computer-literate and regularly encourages us with articles, tips, challenges and prayer requests on e-mail. Incidentally, as if to underline our decision, as Kenny and I sat there talking, someone knocked on our door. Both of us heard it clearly. But when we checked, nobody was there."

They spent two furloughs in Florida at the D&D Missionary Homes: "It was great to have a roomy house on the grounds and we could attend various services and prayer meetings, 'In English!' Lila remembers. Grandma Joseph even came down and stayed a while... long enough so I could have some 20 ladies in for a birthday party for her. One of my very special friends during one of these stays was Phyllis Rilling, who was on leave from Zimbabwe.

"One day Phyllis and I set out for somewhere and we decided that I would drive going and she would take the wheel coming back. Phyllis was driving, and suddenly she decided to make a left turn where she shouldn't have. Immediately from behind came the wailing of a police car siren! Just as she moved to the side of the road to stop, she groaned, 'I forgot my driver's license at home!'

"A young policeman came to her side as she rolled down the window and reiterated what we already knew…that wrong turn! Then he asked, 'May I see your driver's license?' When Phyllis told him her dilemma, he quipped, 'Oh, you've got two counts against you,' and then stepped away to talk on his then-walkie-talkie. My tender-hearted friend was visibly shaken and I'm sure our policeman friend saw that from the beginning. He soon came back and relaxed with his two elbows on the window ledge as he bantered, 'You're really in luck. I can't find a policeman to write up a ticket, so you'll have to listen to me lecture.' He actually seemed to be getting a kick out of it all.

"To try to help or at least offer an excuse, I ventured, 'She's from Africa and I'm from Japan.'

"He had a quick, realistic reply for me: 'I don't care if you're from Timbuktu. She broke the law!'

"Then he good-naturedly motioned for us to drive on without giving us a ticket! I'm sure both of us 'foreigners' in America made double sure we had our driver's licenses when we went out after that!"

## New Carpet

Visiting America was also an opportunity to tend to household business.

"Since our Tokyo house was badly in need of re-carpeting, we visited our friend's factory in California while there and ordered from what he had in stock," recalled Lila. "Being a professional in his trade, he had no trouble getting it shipped to Tokyo at a reasonable price. We rented a truck and picked it up at Yokohama port. Customs officials were also very gracious and helpful. But then came the big problem: Who was going to install it for us? We contacted a recommended company. Their price was $600 per man per day. Two men for three days would do it, we were told. But this was way beyond our budget and more than we paid for the carpet and shipping combined!

"Then I remembered something interesting that had happened just a few days before. My friend JoAnn and I were sitting in a neighborhood coffee shop when a foreign lady (like us!) came in. I had already seen her twice that day. As she was leaving, Jill came over to our table and introduced herself and said that she and her two boys had just moved into the neighborhood from Northern Japan. Very shortly, I searched out her house for a visit and found that she needed stoves, blankets, curtains and other necessities since the belongings she had shipped from her former home hadn't arrived yet. It was November and the nights were cold, so we helped her get the needed items. During our visit, Jill mentioned that she had remodeled ten houses in Seattle while putting her Japanese husband through college. That's when I remembered! If Jill had remodeled ten houses, she had surely laid carpeting. I asked her. 'Yes, I have,' she assured me. 'Laying carpeting is one of the easiest things to do.' I told her our problem. She said, 'If I can be paid for the job what one man would get for a day, I will lay your carpeting.'

"We were overjoyed, and Jill was glad to have the income and to make friends in the neighborhood. She worked with professional skill. I worked right alongside her and learned a lot about carpet laying! What a job to lug the heavy rolls of carpet and padding from the garage. It was sunny weather, so we laid them out in the road in front of our house, which is a cul-de-sac. Inside Jill measured and outside she measured and cut. She knew just how to lift a piece, dig her elbow into it, and pull. How we pulled and rolled. And then we'd drag the right pieces into the right rooms. She ironed splices and carefully laid the rugs so the piling was going in the right direction. Before long it was a finished job and we cleaned up both inside and outside – much to our neighbor's relief.

"Jill and her sons spent Christmas with us, but in March they moved back to Seattle. She was here for only four months, but her three-day job lasted us for years. We're so thankful that we could help her, and then she helped us."

## Driving

Of course, reverse culture shock was sometimes a problem in switching back to the United States from time to time. Lila described the difficulty of driving in two countries:

"I was embarrassed, humiliated, when I finished my first driving exam in Tokyo the instructor said, 'You didn't pass...the driving part.' Hadn't I had a driver's license in America since I was seventeen? Didn't I learn to drive sitting on my brothers' laps? Maybe that was the problem.

So I decided I needed to know what was expected of me and had a tutor take me around the route and instruct me. Then I got my license.

"Driving in two different countries has been a challenge. In Japan we drive on the left side, but in America, it is on the right. Once I went home to help Kimbo in his office and at the end of the first day he dropped by my desk to tell me that he was leaving with a friend. Nonchalantly tossing me his keys, he said I could drive his car home, and off he went.

"Drive his car home? I hadn't driven in America for several years, and surely wasn't ready for California traffic. So I kept working as I pondered what to do. I went out and had supper at a nearby restaurant. Basically stalling. By now it was dark. That was even more challenging. Finally, in desperation, I picked up the phone and called my new daughter-in-law Georgia who, with my son Bobb, lived nearby. I'll never forget that call. Georgia listened to me as I told her I was afraid to drive in America, and then gently but firmly added, 'I'd come and get you, except that Bobb has our car. But any girl who could get herself out to Japan alone can go out and drive that car!' That's all it took. A challenge. I closed the office, went out, jumped into that car and took off.

"For a whole year I dreaded a test I needed to take last year, remembering that Kenny took it the year before,' Lila continued 'He set it all up for me by phone, even finding a worker who would meet me as I drove up to the DMV headquarters for our area. This was a test for those over 70, when their present driver's license expired. There were lots of people there, but I was put in with two others and we listened to a lecture, took turns driving around in the official car, and then were seated on a tall seat in front of a computer. Four tests on that, which as soon as we finished, the computer printouts came flying out, one by one. I noticed that the lady next to me got 'Average.' If she got 'Average,' what would I get? After all, it was in her native language! Imagine my joy when I saw on my paper, 'Excellent,' with the added line 'Your driving is a little better than the average 39 to 59-year-old's. "Very good news to this one who flunked her first test. Maybe it's praying. We rarely take off in Tokyo's traffic without first praying. So much so that when our granddaughter Jacko was about five, and we were leaving in the car one day in California, Kenny said, 'Who's gonna pray?' To which Jacko blurted out, 'We don't pray in America!' But learning the rules and praying are an unbeatable, necessary combination. In America and in Japan."

## Norway

It wasn't until many years of work in Japan had passed that Lila was once again in touch with the language of her childhood. She wrote about a visit Norway:

"Two aunts, my cousin Arlene, and I went on an adventurous trip to the land of my father's parents and Mother's birth," she recalled. "It was June, a beautiful time to be in Norway. Primarily, I was struck with the clean, orderly, attractive homes, often complete with beautiful handmade furniture. This is a land of competent carpenters. Colorful flowering plants graced picturesque windowsills. And long lace-covered tables, artfully set with delicate china, held delicious meals. Fish and salads, I decided, were greatly responsible for the trim physique of these gracious people.

"One night Arlene and I decided to explore the countryside. Though it was nearly 11 p.m., it was still daylight. This was, after all, the other 'Land of the Rising Sun.' We took a winding road up a hill from which we could survey the luscious, green valley where we stayed. It looked as though an outdoor manicurist had just finished his job. In fact, neatness pervaded most every place I saw. I remember even seeing curtains on a barn window!

"But it was after I settled in between the unique, white fluffy down coverlets for sleep that I faced my biggest problem and became very troubled! Why couldn't I speak Norwegian? I understood a lot of what was said and even translated for Arlene, sometimes, but not one word would come out when I needed it. I had been face to face with people, but frustratingly, couldn't pull out the right words and sentences to carry on a conversation. It was then I realized that my Norwegian was buried under not only English, but Japanese, which I use in Tokyo. Still, as I lay quietly night after night, I found that my mind had been activated and was digging up the long-hidden words I knew as a child. I began to form full sentences– there in the darkness where I didn't need them! I finally came to a realistic conclusion: I didn't need to speak Norwegian for my work on an every day basis, but I also reassured myself that if I had six months in Norway, I could become quite proficient in the language."

## Friends and Colleagues

The Josephs were by no means the only missionaries working in Japan. Lila recalls some of the stories of her friends and colleagues.

"One of our missionary friends was a former lawbreaker, from working as a prisoner on a chain gang to doing missionary work in Japan was quite a jump for Ed Martin," wrote Lila. "But two pardons helped him bridge the gap. It's hard to believe that this soft-spoken, white-haired man with the free, easy smile was once a fugitive from justice. A fugitive with bloodhounds on his trail and a bounty on his head!

"Edward, the grandson of a preacher, was thirteen when his home broke up. He went with his father, a builder, and they traveled so much that he went through first grade three times. These were difficult years. Ed hated school. Not so much because of the studies, but because the other kids made so much fun of him. He wore coarse clothes, and he remembers that his lunch pail was an old lard bucket. Lunch, well, that was mostly corn bread and pinto beans. No doubt to make up for all his insecurities, Ed found his niche with a 'bunch of other rough kids.' Together they became a headache for the local police. It wasn't surprising that 'that Martin boy' was finally caught, though actually on a minor offense, and sent to reform school. At this time, Ed's sister, 'who had always tried to do what she could to keep the family together,' he remembers, became a Christian. Her letters to him from then on showed her love and concern for this wayward brother.

"But Ed was not yet ready to change his way of life. Once out of reform school, he started working at a sawmill, drinking and carousing, writing bad checks, and finally stealing a car, which led Ed once again into the arms of the law. This time he was sentenced to four years in the Richmond, Virginia, penitentiary. There he and other prisoners were put on a 6-foot length of trace chain to do roadwork.

"It wasn't many months until Martin, now in his early twenties, and another convict began plotting their escape. The chance came when the two of them were doing roadwork separate from the rest one day. And their one guard had only a .38 revolver in his hip pocket. Faking a shoe problem, which he asked the guard to check, Ed grabbed the man's revolver and he and his companion fled into the Virginia hills. Here the fugitives dodged mountaineers (anxious to get an offered reward) and armed men with bloodhounds for seven days. They were hungry, thirsty, and too tired to resist capture when a squad car caught up with them on a narrow, winding mountain road. Back in prison, Ed found he now had a short step-chain on his legs. He was bitter and hot-tempered.

"Then one day he got a letter from his sister's roommate. She wrote, 'Looking at your picture on your sister's dresser, I'm sure you have many fine qualities. She and I are praying for you, together, every day...'

"Later this girl, Alfreda, visited him and explained to Ed how he could find peace for his troubled heart and life. After she left, alone and in chains, Ed prayed and asked the Lord Jesus to come into his heart. That's when he got his first pardon. The change was dramatic and affected every part of his life. One day the sergeant in charge asked him to preach to the men. He did. A short time later this same sergeant startled Ed one day with, 'Ed, you'll be leaving us next Tuesday.' In explanation, he added, 'You're one of the first men to be paroled under the first parole board in Virginia.' Thirteen men were up for consideration, but only Ed made it. Sometime after this came the second pardon – an absolute pardon from the governor of Virginia!

"Ed married Alfreda soon after he got out of prison, and they spent fifteen years working in Japan as missionaries. Three sons joined their ranks. Then back to Virginia they were involved in prison evangelism. Fitting work for a man who understands prisoners, the man with two pardons."

Lila was also acquainted with a rural Japanese boy who grew up to be a pastor.

"Aside from the fact that he wore dark glasses in the pulpit, Pastor Baba didn't appear different from any other preacher," recalled Lila. "Huskily built, he looked like a football player. Standing there dressed in a neat, brown suit, he spoke with ease and joy. But Pastor Baba was blind. Born in a small country town, he was the youngest of 5 children, but the only child of his father's second wife. When he was a high school freshman, five of the seven family members all got sick at the same time. Only Baba-San and his mother were left to do the farm work and take care of the animals. Baba's day began at 5 a.m. After the farm work was finished, he had a 20-minute bicycle ride, a 20-minute train ride, and a 20-minute walk before he got to school. Then after school there were chores and studies until midnight.

"In a few weeks, the young lad noticed that his right eye was beginning to fail. A visit to a doctor disclosed tuberculosis and he was immediately hospitalized. One night he lay on his bed looking at the light when suddenly everything went black. Without any warning, he lost the sight of both eyes because of tuberculosis-caused hemorrhaging at the base of the eye. Though some sight did return temporarily, he was soon totally blind.

"It was eighteen months before Baba's condition allowed him to go home, but now there seemed to be no meaning to life. He could no longer help on the farm. One day, after a drinking bout, his father made derogatory remarks about his blindness. That night young Baba took his father's military sword and went out into the barn. There he sat down to think a little before committing suicide.

"Many red lights came flashing to the young boy's mind. He knew instinctively that if he took his life tonight, his mother would do the same the next night. He knew he meant a lot to her whose life was so difficult with his father who was from an old warrior family.

"'What if there is life after death?' he wondered. He wasn't sure that there was, but anyway, he better not take a chance. After pondering the situation for some time, Baba made a rational decision: he could die anytime. He would go on living for now. And he would go back to the church that he had once visited and see what they had to say.

"From the following Sunday one, he never missed. Sometimes a friend would take him the four miles by bicycle, and sometimes he would go by bus. Three months after starting to attend regularly, the local butcher who was a keen Christian, led him to the Lord. His life was completely changed for the better and he remained at home for the next two years.

"During this time he developed a creative way to learn Bible verses. He made his way out to meet the children returning from school and ask a child to read to him from the New Testament. As he heard, he memorized. And the child got a piece of candy as a reward.

"In time he was able to go to Bible school, and during that study period, he also learned the techniques of massage and acupuncture. Baba lived alone and did his own shopping and cooking.

"He desperately needed a wife. According to Oriental custom, the right girl was picked. Not only did her other qualities fit, but she had experience taking care of her blind mother! The 'middle man' approached Miss Takahashi about the possibility of marriage to Mr. Baba. She respectfully declined. This was understandable – after all he was blind! But what was her main reason? She felt she didn't measure up to his qualities! The young lady did eventually accept his proposal, and they were married and served faithfully together in service for the Lord Jesus. Jesus called people blind whose eyes were closed to eternal realities. It's better to be blind physically than to be blind spiritually."

Another remarkable Christian worker began her career when most people settle into retirement.

"Retire at 65? Quit work at 80? Dr. Baker wasn't about to do either," remembered Lila. "At an age when most people are at least thinking of taking it easy, she began her missionary career.

"'Grand Central Station' is the way someone just described her small, humble home in the outskirts of Tokyo. Visitors got a warm welcome, and it it's mealtime, a 'farmer's meal'! Very likely they also got what they came for: a treatment, because Dr. Baker was a chiropractor.

"One of fourteen children, Mrs. Baker was born and raised on a farm in Ontario, eight miles from the Michigan border. One vivid childhood memory she had was of her mother sitting in a rocker, nursing a baby and reading the Bible out loud to the rest of the children. With such a big family "there was always a baby," she recalled. There was also lots of Bible. This was to mold her life, but not to take root for many years.

"After one year of nurses' training and a stint working on an Indian reservation, Mrs. Baker took chiropractic training in Iowa. She then set up business in Canada. During the depression it was a flourishing practice. But even then her main purpose was to help people. Some couldn't pay. One lady, whose money she always refused, later left a small amount to her in a will.

"'Because it was good business,' Mrs. Baker went to church. But she got a better incentive when she came to know Jesus Christ as her own Savior during some special meetings. From then on she was not only healing bodies, but reaching hearts as well. Sorrow struck at this time as her husband, shell-shocked from World War I, died after less than two years of marriage.

"When Dr. Baker began to talk of going overseas, it was only natural that people wouldn't understand. Why should she leave a big house, a comfortable practice, friends and family, to venture off to a strange land? And at her age! But the reason was quite simple: She heard the voice of God say to her, 'Go.'

"After closing up shop and selling her modern equipment, Mrs. Baker went – to join her brother in Japan. She thought she was only going to teach the Bible, but word got around that she could help sore backs and aching legs and soon Japanese and foreigners began beating a path to her door. Though her equipment was left behind in Canada, she still had her large, sensitive hands, and a direct line to God, Who, she says, often told her what was wrong and what to do.

"Though she carefully treated everybody who came, Dr. Baker was particularly partial to students from the nearby American Academy. From them she got words of recognition and a clapping ovation at the annual sports' banquets. 'They're my boys,' she proudly declares. After getting banged up in basketball, wrestling or track, they would head for Dr. Baker's. While she massaged their twisted ligaments and put their bones back in place, she talked to them of her best Friend, Jesus, and how practical life with Him was for every day. And she insisted that they listen to her, because, 'I'm not the preacher and I'm not their parents!'

"To Dr. Baker, Jesus Christ was alive. He's her constant Companion. Being with Him every day was her way of life."

## Life and Death

"My Mother just died," a man explained brokenly as Lila rolled down her car window. She had wondered why his car was parked, headed in the wrong direction. She couldn't pass. "Please be patient. She's in that car and we've brought her (body) home from the hospital."

"How well I remember when I heard those words about my dear Mom," recalled Lila. "The phone rang at 4 a.m. I knew instinctively what I'd hear, and sure enough, my oldest brother said, 'Mom just passed away.' Mom had been very sick, so this came as no shock. I had even spent three weeks with her and in fact had been back home only a week. So it was no big deal, right? Wrong! After I hung up, my husband and I prayed and I fell asleep. But when I awakened at 7 o'clock, I was shocked by my feelings. I felt as though someone had grabbed a hold of my heart and twisted it into a knot. Never had I experienced anything like it. But then, never had I lost my Mother, either. Never again would I see the light of day knowing that I had my Mom back in North Dakota. Never again would I go to sleep with the assurance of her prayers. Still, as the day wore on, I realized that Mom was in Heaven with Jesus. Why had I felt so crushed when I first woke up? In my rational thinking I was actually glad that she had gone Home, as it could have been a long drawn out illness. Then I understood: If I didn't have the hope of Heaven, I would indeed be hurting. But I knew where she was and where she wanted so much to go, and I was actually happy. Though I wouldn't see her again down here, there is the great hope of reunion in Heaven. How I wish my unknown friend had this hope for his Mother."

Later, Lila took pen to paper:

Thanks, Jesus, for such a warm welcome!
And for wiping away my tears!
It's been kinda rough.
But now I can see that it was worth it!
I can't believe this dazzling beauty
All around.
The sky. The grass. The flowers.
So vivid. Striking. Breath-taking.
The buildings. And the music.
But mostly I'm glad to see You.
I can never thank You enough for finding me
When I had gone astray.
You turned me around.
It was different from then on.
Hard lots of times.
But I kept reading Your Word
And talking to You.
You kept Your end of the bargain
With peace. Power. Guidance.
I couldn't have gone it alone.
At first everyone made fun of me.
But they gave up.
You kept reminding me that I was in warfare.
That my short stay on earth was not to be a settling in.
I remember once when I was downcast
You led me to Hebrews
Where I read
"For this world is not our home;
We are looking to our everlasting home in heaven."
So here I am. Thank you, Jesus.
I'll say that over and over I know.
But who's that?
Looks like he's waiting for me.
In fact, all those people seem to be waiting.
Oh, I recognize a lot of them.
My family.
Yes, they finally came to You.
One by one.
I'm so anxious to talk to each one!
But Lord, I don't know any of the others.
That one. Waiting.
He was? He was that salesman I shared You with?
And her–the one I gave that tract to?
And witnessed to
At the supermarket? She was crying, I remember.
And those people–our neighbors from our old place.
After we moved I never saw them again.
But I prayed for them.
Sure I remember praying for the people in the airplanes
Going overhead.

> Naturally I didn't hear anything about them
> A lot of them must have come to You.
> But Lord, You know I never went
> To Africa
> Or South America
> Or Japan.
> How could those people be welcoming me?
> Well sure, I prayed and helped the missionaries
> As much as I could
> But still I felt insignificant
> Their job seemed more important.
> Sure, I know they couldn't have done it alone.
> Wow! Everyone's so beautiful
> Really? They weren't when they came?
> Each one seems bubbling over to tell their story
> To me
> And I'm sure I can understand them here!
> But, as happy as I am,
> I'm sad, too.
> I could have helped more
> I could have prayed more
> You've done so much for me
> And I've really done so little.

Familiarity with life and death prompted Lila to contemplate her own mortality. God would sometimes have her lighten up – or at any rate, to trust Him. "Sometimes I think God has a sense of humor in dealing with us," she said. "I had had a medical test and was to go in the next day for the results. I felt the Lord had assured me that all would be well, but still I was nervous. I remember standing near the phone and asking for 'one more' verse of assurance. I'm usually not one to open my Bible and point to a verse. But I just opened my Bible and my eyes fell on, 'I have told you before; would you hear it again?' I closed my Bible, accepting that. And my tests were ok, filling me with praise!"

> Wow! Am I ever glad to be here!
> But I must confess I was surprised that
> You called me.
> You know, I'm not SO old yet.
> I never WALKED on gold before;
> A couple of gold jewelry chains
> and some rings were about it.
> The sky is so blue and clear;
> Beauty and orderliness everywhere.
> I know some of those people over there.
> From our church.

They don't seem to particularly notice me.
Oh well, I didn't pay much attention
to them either.
When we were near each other.
But Jesus, You welcomed me.
I'm glad for that.
I can tell You're happy to have me here.
Still, You seem kinda reserved.
Maybe even sad.
Strange. Some things are dawning on me.
Now I realize that most of the people I
worked with
Won't be here.
I can't believe how utterly self-centered
I was.
I thought it was stalwart to just "live"
like a Christian.
Just warming a pew on Sundays.
I knew I was born-again, I remember the
time I asked You to come into my heart.
But my faith was weak.
I see that now.
Sometimes my Bible lay unread for days.
You know, magazines, papers, TV.
Always beckoning.
And praying!
Well, Lord, you know there can't be many here
because of my prayers.
A few quick "God bless"es while sailing
down the freeway
In between gulps of coffee
Were about it.
There's no excuse either.
I can't remember how many times our pastor
spoke on prayer.
And YOU nudged me, too, Lord.
I was so caught up in day-to-day living.
I planned to pray more.
To help people more.
To ask YOU what You really wanted.
Some day. Some day.
I just forgot how short life can be.
In reality I forgot the purpose You had for me.
Now I see that it wasn't to "get ahead."
Or to keep up with even the
Christian Joneses.
Or to just have the latest "things."
I was to be Your witness.
To take Your place.
That was the last speech You gave to

Your disciples.
And to all Your children.
There's no use asking if I can go back;
Back to help my family.
They were always glad when I kept
my "religion" to myself.
Back to the office.
Don sure isn't ready. Neither is Jack.
Or Carl, for that matter. Or Alice.
I know I could have made all of them listen.
I could have shown more interest.
Been more caring.
There wasn't much "cup of cold water"
business from MY life.
But, like You said, if I did go back
They probably wouldn't listen.
They'd think I was a ghost.
Or deranged.
This is really getting to me, Lord.
Now I know why You were sad
when You greeted me.
I'm glad You said You'd wipe away
our tears.
There wouldn't be enough Kleenex in
all of Heaven
To comfort me and others who've
lived just for ourselves.
Thank you for Praying
This morning I was burdened,
I couldn't even pray,
I said, "My Lord, I don't know why,
But I don't know what to say."
How could I have the wisdom
To know just how to ask,
The problem was too big for me
My need I couldn't mask.
I read my Bible, did my work,
Both listlessly and slow,
I just couldn't reach the Throne Room
For my soul had lost its glow.
So I lifted up my problem,
Gave it all to Him to mend--
How even He could sort it out
I couldn't comprehend.
The day wore on and tasks were done
I move in robot-style,
When suddenly I sensed a change,
From inside I could smile.
Dark pressure was all lifted,
My mind was calm and still,

The change was so dramatic
It went beyond my will.
I pondered what had happened
And then I clearly knew
That God had touched some tender heart
I wonder, was it you?
He'd asked for one to stand up strong
To pray and praise and rout
The enemy who like a flood
Had moved in all about.
"Oh my Father, thank you!
For the one who prayed for me,
Please give that one a special touch
Who served so faithfully"

Chapter 12

# *The Josephs – Today and Beyond*

Lila Joseph never saw her parenting work as anything other than an extension of her work as a missionary. She had a captive congregation of four young boys who would one day become men, and she had come to see that as part of her mission field.

Each of her sons had grown up with differing interests, but each shared a strong commitment to Christ and to the furtherance of his work in various and sundry ways.

Kimbo had developed a ministry to Japanese in the U.S. called Agape House and had parlayed that into a full-time ministry in Japan called the Japan Helpline. In 1987, his work was featured in a documentary on the NHK network in Japan called "The Summer of Agape House," which had brought him acclaim for his work in helping Japanese abroad. Over the next two decades, his work would expand to writing books and lecturing in Japan and eventually take him to Iraq where he worked on behalf of the persecuted Assyrians. He would divide his time between Iraq, Washington DC, and Tokyo, and remained single. He picked up Kenny's long-held interest in research on the hidden Christian history of Japan, and collaborated on a book with his father on the topic.

Bobb, two years Kimbo's junior, married Georgia Withee and eventually settled in suburban Milwaukee, Wisconsin. Together they raised three children, Kerrigan, Reid, and Lydia. Bobb worked primarily in the health insurance field, while Georgia devoted herself to homeschooling their children and later developed an interest in international missions, especially in Sudan. In addition to discipling his children, Bobb devoted much of his time and treasure investing in the youth at his church, leading and mentoring middle and high school students. He comments, "I am so blessed to be a 'third generation' Christian. Not that I inherited my faith, but my personal faith in Christ has the blessing of allowing me to look over the shoulders of a Christian mom and dad, as well as grandparents. And as I have tried to raise and disciple my children in the Lord, I have taken the best of their rearing and added my own."

<u>**Georgia**</u>
Today is Mother's Day!
Set aside for mothers
Young
Older
Old
And I think of you
So special to two little boys who need you so!
And I look back
Before you or I could imagine
God called you
As the only girl in the world
To be my precious son's wife
To stand with him
In encouragement
In help
In sometimes finding a better way
But always in love
You can't imagine
How much you mean to me, also;
Your steadfastness
Kindness
Input, I value
Today I want to put into words how thankful to God
I am
For you
My beloved daughter-in-law
I love you

After graduating from California State University – Fullerton, Jim had gone into real estate while still in college and had co-founded a real estate office, Century 21 Grisham-Joseph, in the early '90s and was the married father of six, Jacqueline, Christopher, Julia, Jamee, Joy and Jase. His wife, the former Cindi Chase, had been a fellow missionary kid in Japan, and she had for many years served as the secretary of the mission. A long-time member of REAP's board of directors, Jim had also co-founded a nonprofit foundation, the James & Cindi Joseph Foundation, whose goal was to help provide funds for Japanese churches. He traveled to Japan often with Century 21 Japan, for which he was a regularly featured guest lecturer.

### Cindi
On Mother's Day...
I don't think you fully realize how special you are to me
I'm so glad that God in His wisdom
Chose you
Equipped you
As the only girl
As the only girl in the world
To be my precious son's wife
To stand with him
In encouragement
In help
In sometimes finding a better way
Stand by him through thick and thin
In love
You do it, and I thank you.
You've given him and us six darling children
No small feat!
But aside from that,
Your kindness, helpfulness, cheerfulness
To me, to us
Are immeasurable
I value your input, suggestions
You're my precious son's wife
My beloved daughter-in-law and
I love you

After graduating from Biola University, Mark began a career in media as a radio and TV news anchor in Japan, an an author and record and film producer in the U.S. He produced the soundtrack for Mel Gibson's "The Passion of The Christ," and worked in the development and marketing of films like The Chronicles of Narnia and others. He also co-founded a church in Tokyo and worked with George Gallup to produce groundbreaking research about spirituality in Japan. He married Kara Berg, the granddaughter of a lay missionary in Japan and they have four children, Anna, Maryn, Maya and Kirra and divide their time between Tokyo and Los Angeles. Mark too has served on the board of Reap since 1986.

### Kara
How could you have dreamed
As you grew up in the Midwest
That your path would lead
To Japan
But then you did grow up
Listening to your dad

And probably your grandparents
Talk about their lives and experiences
On that island so far away!
That summer scholarship stint
To Sendai
Started you on your own Oriental road
It's amazing that you wanted to return
After being introduced to raw fish, seaweed
And roasted fish with the eyes
Looking up at you!
Remember that even your girls balked at that
Out on the farm recently
But the Lord led so clearly
As Aunt Martha asked for your help
That year
Taking a year off from college
Must have been a big decision
But Dad and Mom approved
Little did you know that's when
A young man
Set his eyes on you
Especially in the bleachers at CAJ
Basketball game one night
He saw beauty and character in full bloom
A few more years went by and we had
A gorgeous outdoor wedding
With even Gumbi present
The following years have been busy,
Challenging and rewarding
You are a great helpmate
A good balance for that
Joseph household
And a loving, sensitive mother
To Anna, Maryn, Maya and Kirra
We love you so much and thank God
For your care of us, too
Joining our other precious
Daughters-in-law
Keep looking up and getting
Daily strength
For all those demands on you as
A wife
A homeschool mom
A daughter
And a loved daughter-in-law

Lila had had a vision for her children and the contribution they would one day make in their various fields of endeavor. Each child remembers her walking them to the door and telling them, "Remember whose you are and whom you serve." It was both an encouragement and a warning, to not stray far from the values they were raised with. She was also fond of saying "Do they know how special you are?" which she would later shorten to just "Do they know?" and would often pepper her encouragement to her children with lines like "Just one life will soon be passed, only what's done for Christ will last."

As Kenny, as he continued with his evangelistic work at full-speed, age was beginning to catch up with him, and in 2002 he was finding it difficult to walk. Throughout his life, Kenny had traveled through twenty different countries by planes, trains, ox-carts, and cars. His right hip had begun to bother him badly, and he knew it was time to look for a hip surgeon. After talking to three different doctors, the best surgeon in Japan said that he should go to America for his surgery. Unbeknownst to Kenny, God was in the process of arranging for him to be seen by a world-class hip replacement surgeon.

Mark had recently interviewed the actor Charlton Heston and had noticed a limp. "He said he didn't want to be photographed walking because he was going to have a hip replacement soon," recalled Mark. Mark had kept in touch with Heston in the years following their meeting, and when Kenny talked about needing the operation, Mark called up Heston and asked for the name of the doctor who had performed his operation. "I figured if he was doing Charlton Heston's hips, he'd do a good job on my Dad's," laughed Mark.

"Mark drove me there to his practice in Los Angeles, and I told Dr. Moreland that I'd been referred by Moses," recalled Kenny. "He got a good laugh out of that one and asked Mark to come in and tell him the story." Kenny would eventually have both hips replaced, but then, three years later, another major problem came up – he suffered a minor heart attack.

"It was Christmas, and we had had a service, then a party, and finally in the evening family and friends gathered, all in one day," said Kenny. "During the second day at another evening party, I just felt rising pressure in my head, so I excused myself and went upstairs and lay down. That was evidently when I had the heart attack. Unbeknownst to me, Mark in America was awakened in the night with a vision of me dying and prayed for me."

"It was Christmas Eve when I woke up with a start around 2 a.m.," Mark remembered. "Either I had been dreaming or I was awake when I sensed my father fading away – dying. I remember sensing clearly that as he was fading away, somehow he was remembering his boys with satisfaction – as if we were his greatest accomplishment in life. I woke up with a start and felt a strong impression that I was to pray for him. So I prayed that his life would be spared. And then I went back to sleep. In the morning I wondered what that was about.

"Later I would learn that 5,000 miles away, he was suffering a heart attack that wouldn't even be detected until four days later when the doctor suggested he get on the treadmill. When the doctor found that out, my father remembered the odd feeling he had felt when he excused himself from company and went back to his room feeling discomfort."

"I took the treadmill stress test," said Kenny. "The doctor said that there was up to 80% heart blockage and sent me to an expert for a thallium radioactive test. After the long train ride home, the phone rang and the doctor said just two words: 'heart attack.' Since this was the Seventh Day Adventist Hospital, he recommended that I go to Loma Linda in California, the hospital that had become famous for doing a chimpanzee-human heart transplant."

Bobb sprang into action, making medical arrangements at Loma Linda while Mark picked up Kenny and Lila at the airport and drove them directly from LAX to the hospital. Entering the emergency room with the words "chest pains" got Kenny put into intensive care, and the surgeon recommended open-heart surgery immediately.

"What percentage die during this surgery?" Kenny asked his doctor at Loma Linda. "Twenty percent," he replied.

As the family decided what to do, Mark recalled an earlier conversation he had had with an old friend of Kenny's from college, Ken Beshore who had had stints inserted at Scripps Hospital in San Diego and recommended that Kenny go to see his surgeon, Dr. Tierstein. Kenny did, and posed the same question to him: "3%" was the reply. Kenny and the Joseph family liked those odds better.

"I had only a local anesthetic for this, and Dr. Terstein said that he had 25 doctors up in the balcony watching and learning," Kenny recalled. "'You are on TV for other doctors to watch by remote,' he explained. 'This is the wave of the future.' I could hear and see all that was going on… 'Shall I put in a 5 mm or a 3mm?' They then put in the stints."

Fully recovered, Kenny and Lila returned for more service to Japan.

As the years slipped by, it came time for Kenny and Lila to celebrate their 50th wedding anniversary in Chicago where 100 family members and friends came from Japan, Washington, Oregon, Montana, North

Dakota, Minnesota, Illinois, Iowa, and Wisconsin for the big occasion. The event was planned by Kenny and Lila's daughter-in-law Georgia, and family and friends gathered in the suburbs of Chicago to celebrate the big day. Lila's brothers Orvin and Ray and their family and friends were there among many others, and Kenny's guests included various nieces and nephews. Mark, Jim, and Bobb each spoke a few words about their parents, and two surprise guests of the evening appeared via video tape as taped anniversary greetings from Bill Gaither and Andrae Crouch were played on the screen along with a DVD of highlights of Kenny and Lila's lives.

A recent highlight of Kenny and Lila's year has been an annual trip to Hawaii they take with son Mark and his family, a trip which Mark describes as a slight rebellion against his upbringing:

"Dad made a vow when he was a young man that he would never take a vacation without preaching somewhere, so when we were kids we'd be on vacation somewhere, and of course Dad was on the prowl for somewhere to serve. So once a year we meet up halfway between Los Angeles and Tokyo and help them recharge their batteries, and I try to get him to break that vow whenever possible."

For Kenny, trained as a soldier in God's army, it's still a hard trip to take.

"I want to stay home with the cat, but Lila needs a baggage carrier, so I take up my cross and go along to Hawaii," he laughed. "Mark usually rents a house on the beach, and we get re-acquainted with our four growing granddaughters. It means a time for us to get together when an ocean separates us. In fact, last year, Lila got up from our curtained-off bedroom where we were reading to get something, and as she walked past the couch where two of the girls were sleeping and heard sniffles. Rushing over she asked, 'Are you sick?' With an outburst of weeping one of the girls said, 'Tomorrow you're leaving...' That's always hard. We have thirteen grandchildren and we love them all dearly, but being separated from them is one of the real hardships of missionary life. So we enjoy every opportunity we can to be with them when they come and visit us in Japan."

Looking back now on his many years in Japan, Kenny ponders whether General MacArthur would be pleased with his and Lila's service, in response to his call, a call that ultimately emanated from a higher Being:

"When he arrived in Tokyo after the war, right across the street from the Emperor's palace, Macarthur was the most admired man in Japan,

Kenny recalled. He projected power and strength. Every morning, as he walked into the General Headquarters of SCAP (Supreme Commander Allied Powers), a great crowd would gather on both sides to get a glimpse of Japan's "new emperor." Then after 5:00 p.m., when he would leave, another crowd would come to watch him walk to his car. He once told his staff, 'If you can be away from your desk for three months, stay home. We don't need you.' I believe that we were needed, and we rose to the challenge that God gave us through General Macarthur. I have had two callings from God on my life – Isaiah 61:1 'preach the Good News to the poor,' and Habakkuk 2:1, 'Write the vision and make it plain.' But I would have been lost without my wife Lila, and God knew this. In high school I majored in baseball and woodworking while all the girls majored in typing and home economics. Typing was definitely a 'girl's thing' then. So I praise God for Lila who not only studied typing, but also shorthand. She is probably the only woman in Tokyo who can still take shorthand. And even when I was gone on lengthy evangelistic campaigns, Lila, just like Billy Graham's wife Ruth, was always there for our four boys. "Once I had just gotten home from a campaign, and on my desk was an invitation from Alitalia Airlines for a first class round-trip ticket to Kenya. I said, 'Lila, I just got back and I'm tired. Why don't you take this free flight and go in my place as your wedding anniversary gift.' In her typical answer she said, 'The plane might crash. And you'd have to raise the boys!' I got the message. She wasn't going to take chances on being away from her four boys, even for a free plane trip... All her loving care paid off, and that's the way she sent them off to college...and out into the cruel world after graduation. Now the thirteen grandkids look forward to coming home to Grandma's house and letting her spoil them!"

Through it all, Kenny and Lila have both seen God work in miraculous ways but also experienced deep disappointments. Yet as many of their peers retire, they've continued to make Japan their home into their 80s.

"We've seen more than 5,000 peers come to Japan since 1947 as foreign missionaries or short-term workers, heeding God's calls," Kenny recalled. "Now only eight remain. I impress on our four boys not to believe their own press releases. A good dose of humor helps us keep going. This is unfathomable to those who don't understand what 'living by faith' means. Yet Christian workers go on like sparrows: trusting, living from hand to mouth – from God's hand to our mouth. And looking back on 50 years of God's faithfulness, another song says: 'All I have needed Thy hand has provided, Great is Thy faithfulness, Lord, unto me.' God has provided more than we've needed."

Kenny and Lila always enjoy hosting their grandchildren when they come to see them in Japan. But one recent visit to a local park with Mark's girls nearly ended in catastrophe for Kenny. It was New Year's Eve 2006, when Grandpa Joseph was showing off his bicycling skills to the girls as he pedaled around a local park.

"We had fed the birds and fish, and the girls had played at the park, and we were on our way home when I took a narrow trail to avoid a man and his dog!" Kenny recalled. "That was a big mistake! I fell from my bike onto a lower ridge and Maryn, on the back children's seat went flying also... into a bush! She escaped with no harm, but I hit a stump and my face bled like a stuck pig! Since I'm on blood thinner, it flowed like water! And I had a dislocated shoulder!

"Several buddies come to mind who have had like or worse situations. Cal Junker has lived to tell of his fall while trimming trees, lying on the ground for four hours until his wife Pat came from her bookstore work. Lila's cousin JoAnn's husband, Evangelist Willy Gundersen, was working on his sister's house in Florida when he had a vicious fall, but he continues to preach from his wheelchair, even holding meetings in Norway a couple of times a year...

"So there I was, lying unable to move, especially my left arm. Suddenly, at this quiet time of year, five or six kindly neighbors gathered to help! One lady tore up ahead, catching up with Lila who had gone on ahead yelling, 'Your husband... an accident...' One of the guys had a cell phone (mine wouldn't work), and he called for an ambulance. "The Bible tells us not to despise the day of small things...I came one millimeter away from losing my eye, and a hair's breath from a broken shoulder bone instead of only a dislocated shoulder!

"Ambulance workers in Japan aren't allowed to do anything for the victim, but one man was an expert in stopping bleeding. He quickly wrapped my head as the others worked the phone to find an open emergency hospital on this the busiest time of year. "Five hospitals said 'No,' but one gave us the nod. Would you believe, it was the same hospital where we visited by college friend and fellow-missionary, Buz Reece, a few years ago, and where Mark was taken when he collided with a car – on his motorcycle – and his dented helmet was found across the road. I told the doctor that if he put me in a room with four others, which they usually do, someone would kill me in the night because of my snoring. With a wink and a nod, he said he would check, and they put me into a single room with the expensive balance of zero on my bill instead of $250!

"After having 16 stitches on my face, Mark quipped, 'Hey Dad, get a nose job at the same time!'"

"No such luck," said Kenny. "The dislocated shoulder has been the most painful. The first doctor to begin work on that said he had been in San Francisco for 3 years and he would take care of me! He pulled my arm a couple of times as I literally screamed. 'Relax,' he said. "I couldn't. But the next day another young doctor came in just for me, anesthetized me, and he said it took him 3 seconds to put the shoulder in order. "God is always one step ahead. The enemy threw us a curve ball, but He kept us from serious harm in many ways. Like a Calvinist said, after his Cadillac went over the cliff, 'That might have been predestined before the foundation of the world, but I'm sure glad we got it over with!' "We're so thankful that not only did the Lord protect us from more serious harm, but I am daily getting better and should soon be back to only having to work on the eternal problem of losing weight!"

Today, in their '80s, Kenny and Lila continue to serve God in Tokyo, Japan and unlike nearly all of their contemporaries, have decided to stay in their adopted nation.

"Unless there were some unforeseen circumstance which right now we don't see, we plan to remain here until the Lord calls us Home," Kenny said. "We have good, affordable health care, and I can ride my bike to most necessary appointments. Trains and buses are handy for appointments farther away, and I continue to have openings to speak to continue to tell the Japanese people about Jesus. This year marks four Christian anniversaries for Japan and since my ancestors came in the first century, I speak using my books, *Japan: Country of the Erased Cross* and *Jizo* and *Jesus in Japan* to get my foot in the door. As in the past, this year I expect to get into churches, youth groups, pastor's meetings and others that open up. I would ask prayer for good health to meet these commitments."

He also remains an inspiration to his children:

"Often when faced with a particular challenge or tough decision we think "what would Dad do here," notes son Jim. "Much more than a practical question it is more, 'what would Dad be thinking about this,' 'who would Dad consider to be right,' 'what does Dad think about this person or philosophy.' Life is confusing and challenging and for us four sons having Dad as a lighthouse has been a tremendous asset."

"My Dad was the guy who launched missions for Japan," adds Ken. "He was the first person that ever really began to say that Japanese needed to go out as missionaries, and in that day Japanese didn't hardly have enough money to do anything. He was the one that really proposed the idea that the Bible needed to be rewritten, that they needed to do a new translation. The translation they had was worse than the King James in English. Most Japanese couldn't understand it. My Dad was the one that proposed that they do a new version of the Bible. Now that's really revolutionized the church. In many ways the things they have done over these years have really come into fruition. The very best years of their work here are still ahead."

"Most men would have retired 15 years ago, but Dad remains an active missionary," adds son Bobb. "I don't think he will retire until he is with the Lord in heaven. He accomplished more in his first ten years of ministry than most men accomplish in a lifetime of work. And not only has he reaped a harvest of souls throughout Asia where others have sown, but hundreds of Christian lay leaders have sprung up worldwide from the seeds he has planted in his 50 years of faithful, dedicated service to Christ. If anyone has the following words of Christ awaiting him, it is Dad: "Well done, good and faithful servant" (Mt. 25:21).

"The most important think I have learned from my Father is that in a race, the turtle will usually beat the hare," added Mark. "The hare makes a mad dash, then gets bored or distracted along the way and stops for a nap. But the turtle keeps going and eventually wins. My Dad is like that. While others have given up, he still keeps going just like the hare and eventually prevails."

Lila also keeps a busy schedule at a time when others her age are well into retirement, hosting guests from the U.S., teaching English and Bible classes, writing an advice column on the internet, counseling Japanese and expatriates with family problems and being a grandmother to her 13 beloved grandchildren, albeit from afar, showering them with gifts and encouraging emails.

"With Mom, she was always there, and though a full time missionary with English classes, ladies' meetings and cooking classes, she was always available and made time for us," remembered Bobb. "I remember going out for an evening jog for a mile or two with Mom when I was a teenager. Mom had an amazing Norwegian horse sense to give us lots of freedom to go places and take trips. And as we would leave, she would leave with us the words that would ring in our heads the whole time, 'Remember

Whose you are and Whom you serve.' Mom was the one I went to if I had a problem. She would always listen. She is the living example of the love of Christ to me. No one is more loving and giving than her. If I were asked who most exemplifies Christ on earth, it would be Mom."

"I don't know where we would be today without Mom," adds Mark. "She has been the glue that held our family together and we are all indebted to her."

Both hers and Kenny's lives in Japan has been full of unexpected surprises, joys and sorrows, but through it all, they have clung to God and each other and showed the staying power that comes from a life that is animated by the resurrection power of Jesus Christ.

Kenny summarized that power in his three favorite proverbs: "Winners never quit and quitters never win," "Life is short, death is sure, sin the curse, Christ the cure," and "Only one life will soon be past; only what's done for Christ will last."

For Kenny & Lila Joseph, God's Ambassadors In Japan, the work of spreading the Gospel of Jesus Christ continues, knowing that ultimately they serve Him who sent them to a parched land that is even now, they pray, poised for spiritual revival.

# Appendix 1
## *Spreading the Gospel in Japan*

Many have wondered about the state of Christianity in Japan and why it has never spread like in other Asian countries like South Korea and China. Although Kenny & Lila have toiled for years in a harvest that seemed to not bear much fruit, Kenny often quoted a figure he had heard that 30% of Japanese would, if forced to choose a religion, choose Christianity. Inspired by that and desiring to get more solid data, in 1999, their son Mark teamed with famed pollster George Gallup to commission a poll that would determine those numbers conclusively. With the help of Gallup's Japan staff, they investigated this with an extensive study of the attitudes, values, and beliefs of the people of Japan, with a special focus on the religious and spiritual benefits of the populace that provides some answers. The results surprised many: 4% of Japanese when asked what their religion was, said Christianity.

"In my 50 years of polling, there has been no study that I would consider as important as this one, because it not only provides you with new insight into a fascinating culture (and one that is mysterious to outsiders in some ways), but also because these survey findings point to ways that evangelistic strategies can be put in place," Gallup noted. "As a survey researcher, I am of course dedicated to total objectivity in question wording and other aspects of survey research.

"As a Christian, I am keenly interested in the prospects of spreading the gospel of Jesus Christ in Japan. I believe that the most important discovery one can make in life is the discovery that one can have a personal relationship with Jesus Christ, and it is my constant hope and prayer that every person in the world will come not only to know about Jesus Christ, but to know him as his or her Lord and Savior."

Gallup went on to say that the findings from this extensive and in-depth study "underscore the huge challenges and severe obstacles to the spreading of the gospel, but at the same time, certain shining opportunities," he said.

As indicated, a strategic objective of the study was to try to understand the current thinking of the Japanese people about themselves and the world around them, particularly toward spiritual issues, that would provide a framework for drafting "speaker" sensitive evangelic strategies. By better understanding not only the attitudes of the Japanese people toward spiritual issues (and particularly toward Christianity and Jesus Christ), but also there interests and emotional desires, it is possible to fashion strategies and concerns, and specifically the following.

> 1. Identify the "truth" that Jesus answers for the Japanese people.
> 2. Gain the attention and arouse the interest of the Japanese regarding Christianity and Jesus Christ.
> 3. Appeal to the preserved needs of the Japanese, emotionally and spiritually.
> 4. Point the Japanese toward the gospel as the basis for dealing with all of life.
> 5. Equip Christian leaders and workers in Japan with ways to help them present the gospel effectively to the Japanese people.

Gallup continued, "Before attempting to shed light on each of these areas, I would like to note that, despite the supposed inscrutability of the Japanese, survey respondents were fully open and honest and candid in their response about themselves and their behavior.

"I believe it would be useful, before discussing challenges and opportunities to look at the over all mood of the Japanese people at this time, more than half-century after World War II, as revealed in this study.

"The findings of the study show that the populace is somewhat insular, uncomfortable with diversity and 'outsiders', and possibly, in some small degree, 'racist'. In terms of reaching out to help others, the focus is primarily on one's own family group and not on persons outside these groupings. Broader altruistic motives are not so apparent.

"Most Japanese, judging by their responses to scales on happiness, are neither 'very happy', nor 'very unhappy'. Their responses tend to fall between these two extremes. In earlier Gallup International surveys, responses for many nations fell more heavily in extreme positions than is the case in Japan."

Gallup said that while at least moderately happy, many Japanese seem resigned to being caught up in "the system" or "the cycle of life". There is a degree of fatalism in their somber mood. Teens' perspectives on life tend to a sense of nihilism to an alarming degree. A note of hopelessness is found in the responses to a number of questions. And there is little evidence of eternal hope, although a considerable number do believe in some form of afterlife.

"Like much of the rest of the world, the Japanese tend to take relativistic views on ethical matters," he stated. "There is little belief in 'absolutes' and this is true across the all-generational groups. In the 'hierarchy of crimes' (things that are wrong), those related to economic and family matters far outweigh those related to sexual activity. (David Lewis, author and scholar and well-known expert on Japanese history and culture, points out that the Japanese tend to believe that misdeeds that are self-inflicted and hurt the self are not as bad as those that hurt the group)."

This is a broad-brush picture of the mood of the Japanese population in the twenty-first century, as a backdrop to the challenges and opportunities that present themselves in the efforts to spread the Gospel of Jesus in Japan."

Gallup went on to say, "Perhaps the first and obvious challenge is overcoming the widespread lack of awareness and knowledge among the Japanese regarding Christianity and teachings of Jesus Christ.

"Seven in ten among adults, and half of teens, say they do not know enough about Christianity to express a favorable or unfavorable opinion about this religion.

"Corresponding, seven in ten adults, and half of teens say they do not know enough about the teachings of Jesus in order to give an evaluation. Clearly, all-out efforts should be made to increase the awareness and knowledge of Christianity and the teachings of Jesus Christ – through schools (as part of the study of world religions), television and radio, the internet, newspapers and magazines, churches, and other ways.

"Coupled with these efforts should be those that are directed toward casting Christianity and the teachings of Jesus in a favorable light. Among those who express an opinion on 'Christianity', favorable views outweigh unfavorable ones by a ratio three-to-one. Among teens, however, about equal percentages say favorable or unfavorable. Turning to evaluation of the 'teachings of Jesus', favorable opinion among adults outweighs unfavorable opinion by two-to-one. Among teens, on the other hand, equal proportions say favorable and unfavorable."

Gallup said that these are worrisome findings, both in terms in the lack of knowledge of Christianity and the teachings of Jesus, but also in terms of unfavorable views, particularly among teens.

"It would be important to explore the reasons adults and teens view Christianity and the teachings of Jesus in an unfavorable light, perhaps through in-depth interviews," he said. "The current study, however, shows that most feel one can be Japanese and a Christian at the same time.

"So this does not appear to be a major factor in unfavorable attitudes. Nor are negative views pronounced in terms of 'switching' religions. The majority of the Japanese people claim to have no religion, but this rarely means that they do not have any religious beliefs or practices at all.

"Yet very few in the survey say the spiritual life compare to other aspects of life, is 'extremely important.' Far ahead of spiritual life in importance are family, friends, and education. Relatively few, in addition, place trust in religions leaders.

"In summary, then, we see challenges or obstacles to presenting the Gospel in a number of ways: in the insular feelings and somber mood and feelings of hopelessness of the Japanese people; in the relatively little importance they give to religion compared to other aspects of life, yet at the same time their attraction to other religions (namely Shinto and Buddhism) and 'new religions', as well as their attraction to the paranormal: in their lack of awareness of Christianity and the teachings of Jesus Christ, coupled with a high level of unfavorable views about the same, particularly among young people.

"In some respects there seems to be a solid, impenetrable wall that could prevent the spread of the Gospel in Japan. Are there any possible openings in this wall? Let's look at the survey data in terms of possible opportunities for breaking down this wall of indifference and negativity.

"Certainly an all-out education effort – through the media and the schools and in other ways – could pay dividends.

"Let's look now at the 'bottom line' question: How many Christians are there in Japan? Three in ten adults and two in ten teens claim they have religions. Of adults who have a religion, three-fourths are Buddhists. About one adult in eight describes himself or herself as a 'Christian.'

"Now, let's look at teens. And here we find some stunning and encouraging news, particularly as we look to the immediate value. Two in ten Japanese teenagers claim they have a religion, and one-third of these who do so describe themselves as 'Christians' especially female teenagers. These projections mean that seven percent of the total teenage population of Japan boldly and forthrightly says they are 'Christians.' This percentage projects to an impressive number of young 'new' Christians, excited and energized by their faith."

Gallup went on to say, "Furthermore, despite the fairly high level of indifference to learning more about religion (and specifically, about Christianity and the teachings of Jesus), as many as three in ten adults (and a similar percentage of teens) are interested in learning more about religion, or are already doing so.

"In seeking to reach people for Christ, the Christian message of hope and reassurance in times of darkness would likely be paramount, the survey suggests. Also vital, of course, is the convictions that the teachings of a religion are 'the truth'. In this respect, evangelistic efforts should remind prospective converts of the discovery made by countless numbers of Christians over the ages that often 'faith comes before, not after understanding, as well as the discovery that 'belonging comes before believing'. Relationships should be developed prior to indoctrination. Gallup research shows that people with close friendships in their church are very satisfied with their congregation, less likely to leave their place of worship, and have a strong relationship with God.

"The current study will help those involved in evangelism target particular groups within the population, defined by age, education, sex, and many other characteristics. The sharing of stories and living the example of Jesus in government, in business and in other major sectors of society can, of course, greatly stir hearts among the populace. In China, writes David Aikman, Christianity in the business community is often not discouraged by persons in authority because Christians are found to be honest and law-abiding.

"The challenge to those who seek to spread the Gospel is not only to reach those who do not know Jesus Christ, but also to reach those presently within churches: to remind church members that it is incumbent upon them to share their faith; and to remind Christians of the need to harness the power of their God-given gifts in service to God's Kingdom. Many Christians are unaware of God's plan for their lives. When people discover their gifts and talents, and use these to serve God's purposes, there is no telling what God can accomplish through them."

Gallup said that David Lewis wisely reminds us that evangelistic approaches to the Japanese should be those of "accommodation" rather than "imposition", and that sensitivity should be shown toward the spiritual perspective of the individual being approached.

"An evangelistic program that has proved to be highly effective is the Alpha course, now operating in 150 nations of the world," he said. "Alpha has succeeded because it is responding to a deep hunger for God, coupled with a desire for deeper more meaningful relationships with other people. Alpha is welcoming of all people, regardless of their spiritual of religious perspective, but at the same time is fully faithful to the Gospel of Jesus Christ. Promotion of Alpha or similar programs could bring people to Jesus Christ to a significant extent. It is estimated the 80% of those who take the Alpha course become 'believers'. It is important, however, that the faith of these new Christians be constantly nourished in small Bible study and prayer groups. It has been well said, 'Faith grows best in the presence of faith'.

## Japanese Faith Statistics

"As a missionary kid, I often heard the figure 'one half of one percent' tossed around when it came to identifying the Christian population of Japan," commented Mark Joseph. "I also heard rumors of a poll that allegedly claimed that 35% of Japanese would choose Christianity if they were told they had to choose a religion. I had long thought that any missionary strategy would best be built on a solid foundation of research that captured the heart and soul of the Japanese people.

"I think that George and our entire team have accomplished just that with this survey. The data is insightful, intriguing and often surprising. I was particularly struck by the fact that of the 20% of youth who claimed to have a religion, 36% said they were 'Christians.' That is an almost unimaginable figure. Overall, this survey puts the population of those who call themselves Christians at 4%.

"I can already hear the question: 'Are they truly Christians?' The answer is, of course, nobody can say for sure. Others will rightly conclude that some Japanese are saying yes to all three religions claiming that they're Shinto, Buddhist, and Christian.

"But whether or not these represent true believers or not, it's nonetheless significant that they're willing to tell a Japanese interviewer that they are Christians in such high numbers. It's also interesting to note that while youth claim the Christian faith in almost double the numbers that they claim to be Buddhists and Shintoists, adults are almost exactly the reverse, claiming to be Christians in far fewer numbers."

"George Gallup Jr., America's premiere researcher and pollster, says that this survey is the most important one he has ever participated in, period. He believes, and I believe, that in the data there is a roadmap to the Japanese soul that needs to be explored. We hope that many of you will pick up the baton and use this research in ways that we can't even imagine."

# *Appendix 2*
## *McArthur's Missionaries to McDonalds Missionaries Timeline by Kenny Joseph*

It was the "Macarthur missionaries" who kept asking me to write an eyewitness account of sixty years of post war missions in Japan. I fought this for over five years saying, "Don't ask me; ask the ones who made his rosy to write the history."

But they said, "One by one we've got to get them before they retire." Like the big rush of MacArthur missionaries who came over in 1947-1951...out of the 5000, only 20 remain.

Yet I kept saying, "Let George do it," until I talked to a "long-term" missionary. When I asked him what he knew about the Japan revival in 1955, he said, "Oh, you mean Toyama?"

I said, "No, that was an afterglow, an 'aberration.'" Often when God builds a church, and then Satan puts up a tent next door.

He seemed surprised to hear that there was a genuine revival. That pushed me over the cliff and I said, "OK, I'll write a brief summary of "what my eyes have seen and my ears have heard and my hands have felt."

So I made a list of 30 nation-wide inter-denominational ministries that I saw begin post-war. Each denomination or mission group writes their own histories with names, places and dates of interest only to them and their group. I decided to begin writing a broad range, wide-brush picture that does not pose to be an objective, historical, detached story, but a partly personal, admittedly prejudiced look from the only vantage point I know: my own. This is how I saw and heard it.

### Part One: Post war Ministry Waves

Before and during World War II, the big noise was, "Missionary, go home! You embarrass us as we bring 'peace and prosperity to Asia under Hakko Ichiyu (all Asia under our big Shinto roof)." So all but 10 missionaries left Japan. Germans and Italians could stay under house arrest. Finally what began at Pearl Harbor ended in Hiroshima. Then, beginning in 1945, the expelled missionaries came trickling back. And the ever changing ministry waves began flowing over postwar Japan.

1946: The first wave after the war screamed, "Bring enough food for 5 years!"

1947: The next wave called out "Buy land. Buy land!" Some land was 3 yen (1 cent) a tsubo (36 square feet). Some was 60 (20 cents). A high price was Y3,000 ($9) a tsubo. "Buy land even if you haven't got a church." Mainline churches listened, and others, especially the Southern Baptists, did too. But most evangelicals hesitated. After all, a missionary could live on $125 a month. "Who needs land? And anyhow, Jesus is coming back in 1952!" CIM (China Inland Mission) said, "Just rent. We lost our shirts in Red China!"

1951: The "comity" (let's work this out together) wave rolled in when China fell to Communism and kicked 2,000 missionaries out. Many came to Japan with the word, "Let's not just buy land. Let's also divide the country into comity plans so missionaries don't overlap as they did in China." So the Lutheran Brethren took Akita, CBFMS (Conservative Baptist Foreign Mission Society) took Sendai, CIM took Hokkaido, and so on.

1952: The next big wave was, "Forget buying land. Win souls on the street. Mass evangelism. Evangelize or fossilize!" The big YFC (Youth for Christ) World Congress, the PTL (Pocket Testament League) OMS (Oriental Missionary Society) soul winning crusades and campaigns garnered 33,000 decisions.

1953: Now the shibboleth was, "Follow up, Follow up! Don't run around buying the land up, but follow up." The Navigators came along with follow up offices at YFC, then PBA. Word of Life Press' Every Home Crusade, Emmaus, the Conservative Baptists, and others launched free Bible correspondence courses.

1954: The next big wave was the "indigenous principle" screaming, "Train the Japanese to do the job. Mr. Missionary, don't become a pastor. You just train the Japanese as they did in Korea with the Nevius method and the Three Self program: 'Self supporting, Self propagating and Self teaching.'"

1955: Then came the revival wave. God did send a genuine, sovereign revival to Japan, mostly to and through the missionaries. Revival teams traveled the country holding mini revival prayer meetings. It started to spill over to the Japanese. Some received. Some resisted. When one group tried to "bottle it and sell it with their label," the gentle Holy Spirit flew away.

1956: Next was the "Toyama" phenomenon, which, in the words of one missionary to his colleagues was, "You've sown much and reaped little; now watch us. We'll sow little and reap much," as they and 20 others left their mission organizations and went to Toyama City. There was a genuine move of God there, but with zealous, inept leadership, it withered. Most went back discouraged to their home countries. Two stayed.

1957: The next wave was "Preserve and train the fruit." Little Bible schools and Bible camps sprouted up all over. Some exploded. Many expanded and some later amalgamated.

1959: The following wave was "church planting": If you weren't a "church planting" missionary, you were zilch. So "Para-missions" specializing in needed evangelistic ministries leaned over backwards, stretched and did mental gymnastics to make their ill-prepared missionaries "plant churches" or die trying. Some prevailed. Many quit.

1960: Now "short termers" was the answer to "so few recruits for lifetime career missionaries." It became the next wave. Many came and left. Japanese pastors wailed, "We finally get to know the missionary and he leaves." But some good men and women of this group remained to carry on.

1962: The newest yet oldest wave was, "Teach English. Teach English. They won't come to hear the gospel any more, but they'll come for English and you can give them the gospel." So off flew "Captain English" to the rescue. Despite the potential pitfalls, thousands heard the gospel in this way. (Renowned Japanese evangelist Koji Honda came for cookies, tea and English – in that order! – and found Christ!)

1966: "Muddle through somehow," "S.O.S. (Same Old Stuff)," was the answer to "What's new in missions?"

1987: The "Christian Wedding" wave gains strength and visibility. Some feel it is a Christian "racket" to make money, while others see it as an avenue for "pre-evangelism." With 80 to 100 unsaved in attendance each time (who have never been to church before coming to a Christian wedding chapel), tens of thousands each year hear a minimum gospel presentation during the wedding ceremony. Bibles and tracts are given away to the bridal couple and other guests. The entire message and ceremony is videotaped and is replayed to hundreds of friends for years to come.

1988: Another new wave is the "tent-making" entrepreneur evangelist (an entrepreneur being one who assumes the risk and management of a work; enterpriser, undertaker). These self-supporting, pay-your-own-way-business-for-Jesus maverick missionaries ("a recalcitrant individual who bolts his group and initiates an independent course-after Mr. S.A. Maverick, a Texas cattle owner who did not brand his calves!") have valiant hopes. But after a 7 a.m. to 7 p.m. work and commute, dinner, TV and sleep beckon. Still, there's Sunday! And they reach some people the preachers can't.

Through it all for the past 60 years, long-term missionaries have seen these and other waves come and go. We admit that the Holy Spirit has used many methods and men and avenues in Japan. Each has left an impact – some more than others. Only eternity will reveal the final results. God never orders a great seed sowing unless he plans a great harvest!

# *Appendix 3*
## *Keikyo: Rediscovering Japan's Christian Roots*

An area of Kenny's work that has been powerfully picked up by his son Ken has been Kenny's study of the Christian roots of Japan. Kenny has long believed, despite commonly accepted wisdom to the contrary, that Christianity came to Japan shortly after the death of Christ, and not centuries later as asserted by many historians. The following article was written by Ken.

"The Assyrian Empire ended in 612 BC and the Assyrian Monarchy was abolished in 300 AD. It is them that, according to Yale's Kenneth Scott Lautorette became 'The largest Missionary Force in History,' carrying the gospel as far as China and Japan, with recent discoveries confirming a presence as early as 52 AD in China," noted Ken who has done extensive research in the area. "It is the Assyrians that still speak Aramaic, the language that Jesus spoke. The recent discovery – which according to the locals is "old news" – near the city of Sian, in Central China, has dramatically changed the historical record of China and Asia. Asia, China and Japan in particular, are thought of as predominately Buddhist areas. The record of the Church is very limited throughout Asia with the exception of The Philippines and Korea. As amazing as it may seem, the oldest Christian site in Asia has been discovered dating back to 638 AD. The site which is near the ancient Chinese capital of Sian has shattered the previous understanding of the role of Christianity in China, Japan and Asia.

The Nestorian Monument, a stone tablet in the city of Sian which was discovered in the 1600s was the only testimony to Christianity in China. What was always a puzzle was that it clearly stated that "monasteries abound in a hundred cities." This monument which is often called the "Rosetta Stone" of Christianity in Asia was the only proof of this past. The discovery of the Christian site has dramatically changed all this. The Church is in the center of the Imperial area of the Tang Dynasty and its location is what is particularly bringing amazement to experts on the Silk Road. With the Church in the center of the imperial area it confirms for the first time the stories that have long been passed down and appear frequently in Chinese narratives which tell of a major Church in China in the Tang Dynasty from 618-877. According to "The Cross and The Lotus" by Lee Shiu Keung in 635, Bishop Alopen Abraham from The Church of the East began his mission in Chang Ang, present day Sian. An even earlier Christianity which had been brought directly to Sian by the apostle Thomas in 64 AD had for the most part died out due to the closing of the Silk Road by the people of Turkestan. In 630, however the Silk Road was restored and travel between the East and the West resumed.

The Tang Dynasty was a very special period in Chinese history where there was a broad policy of tolerance and interest in fostering foreign religions. In 638 Alopen completed the first Christian book in Chinese, "The Sutra of Jesus the Messiah." In this book it was carefully argued that Christianity was part of China's ancient tradition. In appreciation for the good of the Eastern Christians an Imperial Decree was proclaimed that provided for the first building of a Church. Later on The Church of the East was favored by another Imperial decree and Alopen was promoted to Great Spiritual Lord, Protector of the Empire, Metropolitan of Chang An. The Church encountered ups and downs but following a period of persecution falling the fall of the Tang Dynasty grew again in the 13th and 14th Centuries and were again so respected by the Emperor that according to the ancient Chinese document the Yuan Shi, Chapter 89, the Governor appointed a special officer to take charge of the affairs of the Church of the East with the second high-test rank in China. This office was solely to manage the affairs of the many bishops, priests, monks and to see that all the sacraments were carefully observed. According to the Yuan Shi there were 72 Church of the East monasteries during the period 1289 to 1320 not to mention the multitude of churches and believers.

What happened? With the complete restoration of the Silk Road in the 13th Century Pope Nicholas IV sent John of Montecorvino to the Chinese court. The Priests of The Church of the East in the Imperial Court and the Franciscan's did no get along. Once again under the Mongols there was a period of great religious toleration. This was again a period of great growth for the Church in China, but this again came to an end in 1369 when communications with the world were cut off with the decline of the Mongol Empire. This hitherto almost unknown period in the Church in China and Asia testify to the great growth of the Church. What does this mean today? First, it completely alters the previously thought ideas about Asia, in particular China and neighboring Japan. Previously it was thought that Christianity was a small part of the picture, but with the recent discovery of a Church in the center of the Imperial Compound, it can be clearly said that Christianity as it clearly stated in the Nestorian Monument was a central part of China at that time and there were Churches throughout China and Asia. Second, it clearly puts Eastern Christianity as a "Chinese" and "Asian" religion. Particularly with an Asia that is very conscious of the Colonial eras in which the conquering was done in the name of Western Christianity, this indigenous form of Christianity which although properly Christian, was very democratic and admired.

Why, some ask is it so important to find history? The answer is quite simple. In Asia, history counts. To present individuals and whole areas with a gospel that has no connection with them is extremely difficult, but to present the Gospel to them as the faith of their fathers calling them not to accept a new religion but to "go back" is completely different. Further, while many countries in the regions actively discourage "Western religions" the Church of the East is clearly an "ancient" and "Asian" religion, and it enjoys great support and respect.

It points to the simple fact that when Jesus commanded the disciples to go to the "ends of the earth" they went and the Gospel was proclaimed and the Church expanded to India in 51 AD, China in 64 AD, and Japan about 70 AD, and then throughout the world. The proclamation of the Gospel to those who have "never heard" as opposed to those who are descended from those who once knew, brings the dual blessings of pride in ones past as well as the inherited prayers of previous generations.

 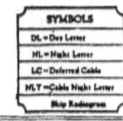

CAY006 LONG GOVT DL PD=WUX CHICAGO ILL 13 617A=
THE GIDEONS INTERNATIONAL=

I HAVE MANY TIMES PUBLICLY STATED MY FIRM BELIEF THAT
CHRISTIANITY OFFERS TO JAPANESE PEOPLE SURE AND STABLE
FOUNDATION ON WHICH TO BUILD A DEMOCRATIC NATION. JAPANESE
PEOPLE THEMSELVES ARE BECOMING INCREASINGLY AWARE OF
FUNDAMENTAL VALUES OF CHRISTIAN RELIGION AND APPRECIATIVE OF
ITS SPIRITUAL AND MORAL BLESSING. YOUR ASSISTANCE WILL BE
OF INESTIMABLE VALUE. COPIES OF HOLY SCRIPTURES, ESPECIALLY
NEW TESTAMENTS, BOTH ENGLISH AND JAPANESE LANGUAGE VERSIONS,
ARE ESSENTIAL FOR SUCCESS OF CHRISTIAN MOVEMENT AS BASIS
FOR STUDY AND ACCEPTANCE OF THE FAITH. JAPANESE TEXTS MORE
IN DEMAND AND CAN BE READ WITH FULLER COMPREHENSION BY MORE
PEOPLE. YOUR REPRESENTATIVE WELCOME TO COME TO JAPAN AS
MISSIONARY TO MAKE FIRSTHAND SURVEY OF SITUATION.
INFORMATION BEING FURNISHED YOU BY AIRMAIL WILL BE HELPFUL
FOR YOUR PLANNING. I ASSURE YOU OF MY DEEP APPRECIATION OF
YOUR INTEREST IN SPIRITUAL REHABILITATION OF JAPANESE
PEOPLE=
      DOUGLAS MACARTHUR   SCAP, TOKYO JAPAN 130835Z.

# *About the Author*

Dan Wooding, 68, is an award winning British author, journalist and broadcaster now living in Southern California with his wife Norma to whom he has been married for 45 years. While living in London, he worked as a senior reporter with some of the UK's top circulation newspapers and also did radio interviews for the BBC. After moving to the United States in 1982, he was, for ten years, a commentator, on the UPI Radio Network in Washington, DC, and now hosts the weekly "Front Page Radio" show on KWVE 107.9 FM in Southern California, which is also carried on the Calvary Radio Network throughout the United States. The program is also aired in Great Britain, Belize and South Africa. Dan is the founder and international director of ASSIST (Aid to Special Saints in Strategic Times) and the ASSIST News Service (ANS) and the author of numerous books, the latest of which is his autobiography, "From Tabloid to Truth" which carries a foreword by Brother Andrew and an introduction by rock keyboard legend, Rick Wakeman.

www.ingramcontent.com/pod-product-compliance
Lightning Source LLC
LaVergne TN
LVHW091545060526
838200LV00036B/715